Matilda Betham-Edwards

Through Spain to the Sahara

Matilda Betham-Edwards

Through Spain to the Sahara

ISBN/EAN: 9783743317291

Manufactured in Europe, USA, Canada, Australia, Japa

Cover: Foto ©Andreas Hilbeck / pixelio.de

Manufactured and distributed by brebook publishing software (www.brebook.com)

Matilda Betham-Edwards

Through Spain to the Sahara

CONTENTS.

CHAPTER I.

SUNDAY AT TOURS — LA COLONIE DE METTRAY — BEAUTIFUL DORDOGNE — A FRENCH PARSONAGE — THROUGH THE LANDES — THE SOPORIFIC EFFECTS OF ARCACHON . . . 1

CHAPTER II.

THE MISCONCEPTIONS OF LUGGAGE — THE COMFORTS OF SPANISH RAILWAY TRAVELLING — OUR LIBRARY — FROM THE TROPICS TO THE STEPPES — GREGORIA AND ISIDORA — JOURNEY TO MADRID 24

CHAPTER III.

THE GAIETY OF MADRID — THE IMPERATIVENESS OF TEETOTALISM THERE — THE QUEEN AND THE ROYAL BIRTHDAY — ROADS AND RIVER-BANKS — APROPOS OF BULLS 41

CHAPTER IV.

VELASQUEZ, THE PAINTER OF MEN—MURILLO, THE PAINTER OF ANGELS—RIBERA, THE PAINTER OF INQUISITORS—ZURBARAN, THE PAINTER OF MONKS—GOJA, THE HOFFMANN OF SPANISH ART—THE QUIETUDE OF THE GALLERIES . . 63

CHAPTER V.

A LEAR OF CITIES—GOTHIC, ROMAN, AND MOORISH REMAINS—COMMENTARIES ON STREET'S GOTHIC ARCHITECTURE AND ON TOLEDAN LANDLORDS—TILES, AND A DISCOURSE THEREON . 81

CHAPTER VI.

A MIDNIGHT HALT—ITS CHARMS AND COUNTER-CHARMS—DON QUIXOTE'S COUNTRY—THE SLEEP AT CORDOVA—WE WAKE IN THE EAST—SHOPPING 108

CHAPTER VII.

"THE SWEETEST MORSEL OF THE PENINSULA"—COB-WALLS OR THE HOUSE THAT CAIN BUILT—PALMS—THE GOOD WORKS OF THE SISTERS—THE PRIESTS AND THE PEOPLE—IS SPAIN UTOPIA? . . . 134

CHAPTER VIII.

"A BOAT, A BOAT, MY KINGDOM FOR A BOAT!"—THE VICTIMS OF A TUNNY-FISH—SENOR BENSAKEN SPEAKS HIS MIND, AND WE ARE REPROVED—RUNNING WATERS—HOWLINGS OF TARSHISH—PEPA'S FAMILY . . . 158

CHAPTER IX.

DAYS IN THE ALHAMBRA—THE GRANDEUR WITHOUT AND THE BEAUTY WITHIN—"CIELED WITH CEDAR, AND PAINTED WITH VERMILION"—AZULEJOS AND ARTESONADOS—MR. OWEN JONES' HANDBOOK 175

CHAPTER X.

PIGS, VULGAR AND ARISTOCRATIC—THE GIPSY CAPTAIN BEWITCHES US—WE GO DOWN TO THE POTTER'S HOUSE—A FAMILY DANCE—AN AWFUL DISCOVERY—A BOOKSELLER OF TARSHISH . 187

CHAPTER XI.

THE ARCHBISHOP BLESSES THE ENGINE, AND WE HELP HIM—DELIGHTFUL LOJA—A FUNNY DINNER—STARLIGHT, TWILIGHT, MORNING 209

CHAPTER XII.

WE GET TO ALGECIRAS, AND ARE MADE WRETCHED—THE FAT SPANIARD AND THE LEAN ENGLISHMAN—A RED-LETTER DAY AT GIBRALTAR—THE LIGHTS—ADIEU TO EUROPE . 222

CHAPTER XIII.

A BRIDAL PARTY—HORRIBLE STORIES—A LONG DAY—THE CAID AND THE DRIVER—A NEW ATMOSPHERE—TCLEMCEN . 239

CHAPTER XIV.

TCLEMCEN, THE GRANADA OF THE WEST—ARAB POETS—THE CHILDREN—THE MOKBARA—SIDI BOU MEDIN—MANSOURA—PHILO-ARABES—TEMPTATIONS IN TCLEMCEN . . 253

CHAPTER XV.

HOSPITABLE ORAN—CHRISTMAS DAY AT LE SIG—THE LAST OF THE PHALANSTERIANS — BARRAGES — THE MALARIA — ABD-EL-KADER'S MOSQUE—SAIDA 270

CHAPTER XVI.

OPINIONS, CIVIL AND MILITARY—A LOOK TOWARDS THE SAHARA—WILD GEESE—OUR SPAHIS, AND THE CARE THEY TAKE OF US—A NORMANDY APPLE-ORCHARD IN AFRICA—NEW YEAR'S DAY 287

CHAPTER XVII.

RAIN — HOW TO CARRY ONE'S WARDROBE — AN ENGLISH LADY'S OPINIONS ON THE ARABS—WILD BIRDS—THE EARTHQUAKE 304

CHAPTER I.

SUNDAY AT TOURS.—LA COLONIE DE METTRAY.—BEAUTIFUL DORDOGNE.—A FRENCH PARSONAGE.—THROUGH THE LANDES.—THE SOPORIFIC EFFECTS OF ARCACHON.

ON a golden autumn afternoon we found ourselves in the old city of Tours, bound for Spain and the enchanted lands lying north of the Great Sahara. Pleasant it was to look backward and forward; backward to the busy life in England, forward to the bright holiday of travel, repeating to ourselves again and again the sentiment, if not the words, of Catullus :—

> " Jam mens prætrepidans avet vagari,
> Jam læti studio pedes vigescunt,
> Oh! dulces comitum, valete, coetus,
> Longe quos simul a domo profectus
> Diversæ variæ viæ reportant."

We were to be made so much richer and so much

wiser by the experiences of the next few weeks; a new country was about to be mapped out on our chart: we were to speak another language, breathe another atmosphere, feel the influences of another religion. For the present we were at home, among French faces and French voices; and, however impatient we might be to reach the wonderful country lying beyond the Pyrenees, we could but willingly linger in these lovely border-lands.

It was Sunday, and our hearts were yet full of the tender beauty of the region through which we had come, when we reached Tours, and joined the stream of church-goers. The Cathedral on that glowing autumn afternoon was a sight to remember, standing as it did against a bright blue sky, with a rosy flush of sunset upon its spires. Nothing can be richer than the façade, and yet so simple is the construction as a whole, that one comes away with a clear idea of it in every part. We lingered in the light for a little, and then went in. A mediæval-looking priest, with shaven head, was preaching to a crowd of reverent peasants — and we listened, no less reverent, to a sermon that might have been preached hundreds of years ago. The preacher had a melancholy, monastic face, and a fervid eloquence that would, perhaps, have stirred up any other congregation, though none could have been more devout than these simple-hearted vintagers and farmers. We stayed till the sermon drew to a close, and then went on by train to Mettray.

It was at Tours that the Saracens were driven back, and it seemed to us a good starting-point for a journey which had for one of its objects the study of Moorish monuments in Spain. We amused ourselves with speculating upon the condition of Europe had the Saracens succeeded at Tours. But for that defeat, we might have had now—who knows?—a Caliphate at Marseilles, and, perhaps, a Cordova at Oxford. But, no; climate, if not Anglo-Saxon spirit, would have driven the sunshine-loving Moors from our island, so that, even in dreams we cannot spread Islamism farther than the Rhine,—which is a consolation to good churchmen and patriots!

I purpose narrating our journey from the very

beginning, because on our way from Paris to Bayonne we made two excursions which I should strongly recommend to every one; firstly, to the great agricultural Reformatory of Mettray, and secondly, to the Protestant Orphanages of La Force in the province of La Dordogne. We reached Mettray in about twenty minutes. Such a sweet, peaceful, little spot lying in the heart of the wine-country! The village postman conducted us, through a dusky winding road that was all a-twitter with the twilight songs of birds, to a large Swiss cottage that proved to be an inn, where we slept as if we had lived there all our lives.

The chirping of the birds woke us early, and we hastened to pay our visit to *la Colonie*, as the great Reformatory is cheerfully and properly called. For Mettray is neither more nor less than a collection of farms and factories, carried on by such waifs and strays of society as its humane founders have been able to snatch from destruction. Once having entered the gates, the whole system of the place suggested itself to us. To our right, to our left, peeped from the trees pretty-looking farm-buildings and workshops, all resounding with the noise of the wheel, the hammer, the saw, and the turning-lathe, and made sunny and pleasant with trellised vines and well-kept gardens. Every place was orderly, quiet, and cheerful; and, as we passed along, the young farmers and artisans greeted us, if not with blithe, at least with contented faces. Leaving our letters of introduction at the porter's lodge, we made a survey of the place accompanied by an intelligent person employed as superintendent of the boys. Our first object of interest—for we knew something of agriculture ourselves—was the farm; and here was meat and drink to delight the most orthodox Suffolk farmer going. Beautifully stalled bullocks; pigs, cleanly littered or scampering about, of the proper breed, small of bone, long of body, sleek of skin; stores of grain, of root, and of forage; a good supply of modern farm-implements,—in fine, every accessory to good farming on a miniature scale.

Then we passed on to the workshops, which were like so many hives, only a little quiet, considering the age of the bees. Some of these workmen, in blue blouses and wooden shoes, were mere mannikins of six or seven years old; but if to a stranger the discipline appears a little hard, it must be remembered that each and all have been snatched from the discipline of prison. All these eight hundred boys, whom we saw working under such kind and pitiful supervision, were, in fact, criminals, and well for them and for society that the benevolent founders of Mettray had come to the rescue in time.

The type of physiognomy was strikingly low, narrow forehead, flat skull, vicious mouth, and deep-set, cunning eyes, which would seem as if the physiognomy, as well as the propensity, of vice, is hereditary; for most of these children were the offspring of crime and vagabondage. The lowest type of face, intellectually as well as morally speaking, was not that of the Parisian, but that of the peasant; and it interested us to find that, as a rule, the best-behaved Mettray boys were also the most intelligent. Each boy is at liberty to follow the trade he likes best, and, oddly enough, the favourite one seems to be that of tailoring. We found in the little world of

Mettray, as in the great world beyond, that every one had fallen naturally into his place. The stupid boys loved to follow the plough, the inventive to handle the carpenters' tools, the lovers of nature to tend the cattle, the effeminate to cook the dinners, the enterprising to manage the farm. All are at liberty, also, to attend evening classes, and, as a reward of merit, to learn music.

"If it were not for that," said the good-natured superintendent to us, "we should fancy Mettray a prison. The boys are summoned to work by music every day, and sing at chapel on Sunday. Oh! if you only knew how they enjoy it!"

We could easily understand this, for when the little band of musicians was summoned to give us a concert, nothing could equal the alacrity with which the summons was obeyed. There was a good deal of shyness and excitement at first, but a real, hearty relish of the music as soon as it began, perfectly delightful to witness. The superior intelligence, I might almost go so far as to use the word refinement, of these boys from their fellows, was quite remarkable. Not one of them had a brutish or brutal look. When the concert was over, we went into the chapel and the class-room. The latter was decorated with pictures, maps, and " honourable mentions," of former Mettray boys, who had fought in the Crimea, in Algeria, in Mexico. Portraits of the Emperor were not wanting, nor, indeed, anything to encourage these poor little outcasts to love their country, to go out into the world and to make men of themselves. I was pleased to find the wards and dormitories also decorated with pictures and medallions, the highly-prized rewards of good conduct; while the outside of every building was trellised with grapes, a more material reward, not of special good conduct, but of indiscriminate industry.

"The grapes belong to the boys and are divided when ripe," said our guide; "it's very pleasant to see that not a bunch is surreptitiously touched, and that every one gets his share at the proper time. But only consider what a saint we have at our head! Who could help growing better with such an example as Monsieur De M—— before him?"

The gentleman in question is the founder of Mettray, and spends all his time and thought among the outcast children of his adoption. It was quite touching to find how he had leavened the whole lump of this little society with his own goodness; and very proud and happy we felt at receiving an invitation to breakfast with him and his daughter the Countess B———. But before speaking of this pleasant breakfast, I must mention one of the most curious features in the *Colonie* of Mettray. Every one has seen in *The Times* the advertisement of some persistent and philanthropic clergyman, who undertakes to make unmanageable boys perfectly tractable and gentlemanly in a few months' time. But they manage these things better in France, as will be seen by the way in which the benevolent supporter of Mettray has effectually supplied the want of such obliging clergymen.

Monsieur De M———'s pet project is what he calls, "La maison paternelle,"—in other words, a refined sort of prison for the refractory sons of gentlemen. The prison is attractive enough outwardly, and looks like a pretty Swiss house, but, in spite of carpets and curtains, the interior is gloomy. We were conducted all over the building, and our guide was at great pains to give us a clear idea of what was, evidently, his pet project. Unruly boys are sent here under the charge of a tutor for terms of one, two, or more months; they are kept to hard study, and during their hours of work the key of their cells is turned upon them, and their behaviour is watched by the tutor through a tiny pane of glass let in the doors. As a reward of good conduct, more cheerful kinds of cells looking on to the garden and adorned with pictures are given, but the peep-hole and the key are never wanting.

"It is an admirable institution, this *maison paternelle*," I said, a little doubtfully; "and must relieve parents of a good deal of responsibility; but it would never do to lock up English boys, and watch them at their lessons through a peep-hole."

The superintendent smiled.

"We had one English boy here once——" he said, and then stopped short.

"Well, and how did it answer in that solitary case?"

"Very ill, I assure you. He burst open the lock, refused to work, defied his tutor,—in fine, all but created a mutiny, and heartily glad were we to get rid of him."

It was now ten o'clock, Monsieur De M——'s breakfast hour, and we were conducted to the simple yet elegant house which he inhabits among his adopted children. We found a man past middle age, exquisitely polished in manner, enthusiastic almost to the pitch of inspiration, kindly, grave, cheerful. It was worth the journey from Paris to make such an acquaintance. The Countess, too, was charming, and seemed almost as interested in the little world of Mettray as her father. But to talk with Monsieur De M—— was like being transported into a new and purer world. He seemed gifted with unselfishness as with a sixth sense, and handled sin and the sorrow born of it tenderly and trustfully as none but the Apostles of humanity can.

But even good and great men have their hobbies, and the hobby of M. De M—— was his *maison paternelle.** So earnest and eloquent, indeed, was he in the cause that he all but converted us to the belief in bars and bolts as a cure for

---

* " La puissance paternelle, il faut le reconnaître, perd chaque jour, de son autorité. L'esprit d'independance qui se manifeste de plus en plus dans la société, a pénétré jusque dans la famille. Les tendances de la jeunesse à devancer l'époque de son émancipation devaient naturellement amener ce triste résultat, dont les fatales conséquences ne nous ont été que trop souvent révelées pendant l'exercice de nos fonctions de magistrat. Nous avons donc considéré comme un devoir de conscience de remédier à un tel état de choses, en cherchant les moyens de ramener dans la voie du bien les enfants que l'inexpérience de l'âge ou la précocité des inclinaisons mauvaises conduisaient à s'en écarter. Tel est le but que nous avons cru pouvoir atteindre en fondant une nouvelle institution, véritable collége de répression, comme l'a si bien definie Monseigneur l'Evêque d'Orléans, où des jeunes gens sont placés sous une discipline sévère, pendant le temps nécessaire pour réprimer chez eux l'esprit d'insubordination et les fâcheux penchants qu'ils ont manifestés. N'ayant entre eux aucun rapport, ils n'ont point à subir l'influence d'un contact trop souvent pernicieux. (Le système de la séparation est si rigoureusement observé que les élèves ne sauraient s'apercevoir, même à la chapelle.) Leur instruction se poursuit donc dans les conditions les plus favorables, les études ne sont pas interrompues; les élèves peuvent même continuer à composer, comme par le passé, avec leurs condisciples au moyen des devoirs que nous sont communiqués par leurs anciens professeurs. De cette manière, l'émulation ne se ralentit pas, et, accompli en dehors

naughtiness. He gave us a prospectus of the establishment, which I transcribe below, and which will give the reader a truer idea of its spirit than any comments of mine. It is incontestable

de toute distraction, le travail est des plus profitables. On enseigne aussi les sciences, les langues étrangères, et les arts d'agrément. Avant la fondation de notre maison, le seul parti extrême auquel les chefs d'institution pussent recourir, était l'expulsion du collége ; cette mesure compromettait l'avenir de l'enfant sans le guères de ses mauvais penchants. D'ailleurs la crainte de l'expulsion était inefficace à ramener dans le desir certaines élèves insubordonnés qui faisaient tous leurs efforts pour provoquer un renvoi. L'approche des vacances multiplie les demandes d'admission de la part des familles. Qui ne comprend le danger qu'il y aurait à récompenser un enfant, qui, pendant toute l'année, n'a mérité que des reproches ? et cependant les parents se résigneraient difficilement à transformer leur maison en un lieu de répression, au moment où tout est joie et fête dans la famille, surtout lorsqu'il s'y trouve d'autres enfants dont on n'a qu'à se louer. . . . . Les heureux résultats obtenues depuis plus de dix ans nous ont déterminé à signaler aux parents les incontestables services que notre fondation est appelée à leur rendre. Nous ne saurions trop recommander aux familles d'apporter la plus grande sollicitude à combattre de bonne heure chez l'enfant toute la tendance à l'indiscipline et à la paresse, dont les conséquences sont beaucoup plus graves qu'on ne serait porté à le croire. On commence par être mauvais élève, on finit par devenir mauvais sujet."

that, however antagonistic such a system may be to our English notions, it has hitherto worked well in France.

But a breakfast—even a French breakfast of twenty dishes—soon comes to an end, and we found ourselves compelled to quit our hospitable entertainer, just as we were fairly seizing the spirit of his great undertaking. Reluctantly we bade adieu to the peaceful asylum of Mettray, and sauntered through the vineyards to the railway station. It looked a lovely land to live in, especially now, when it lay bathed in the rosy splendour of autumn. Here and there, a stately old chateau peeped from amidst the chestnut-trees, or we came upon a grave peasant, who might have been one of George Sand's heroes, driving his team across a sweet-smelling beet-field. As we passed the village church, a wedding party issued from the gate. The bride, who was a brunette, looked very handsome in her bright purple dress and orange-wreath, and the bridegroom and whole happy party saluted us. We ought to have stopped to wish them joy, but we didn't think of it in time; and when we turned back, ashamed of our English shyness, the white ribbons of the last bridesmaid were disappearing round the corner. " Mon Dieu, those English are cold-hearted people!" I can hear these honest peasants say over their wedding-feast. " They meet our Jeanne and her Jeannot coming from church and never stop to utter a blessing !"

Pretty Jeanne! I hope that our negligence may prove no ill omen to her after-life. It was downright shyness, and not ill nature, on our part, after all.

From Mettray we proceeded by rail to Tours, and on to Libourne, a pleasant and picturesque bit of rail, spoiled in this instance, however, by the late inundations of the Loire. One reads of these inundations, and laments over them at home, but is far from realising the actual state of things without personal experience. Horace's ode on the overflowing of the Tiber gives a more approximate idea of the prevailing ruin and dismay than anything; and my fellow-traveller (we don't intend quoting Latin all the way) broke out with :—

> " Piscium et summa genus hæsit ulmo,
> Nota quæ sedes fuerat columbis ;
> Et superjecto pavidæ natârunt
> Æquore damæ."

We travelled all the way from Tours to Libourne with an English gentlemen, who gave us horrifying accounts of the Spanish inns.

"Sleep at Cordova!" he uttered, with a positive shriek of dismay; "sleep at Cordova! I warn you not to attempt it; I forbid you to attempt it. It's awful! it's disgusting! it's impossible! I was travelling in Spain with my wife a year ago, and we stayed a night at Cordova. The beds and floors were alive with vermin, and, as a last resource of sleeplessness and disgust, we betook ourselves to arm-chairs and railway rugs. Whatever you do, don't sleep at Cordova."

And so kindly anxious was he for our comfort that, when he alighted at some half-way station between Tours and Libourne, he ran back to the carriage just as the train was moving off and called out, " Don't sleep at Cordova."

We took the diligence to St. Foy next day,

that being the nearest post-town to La Force. It was not a comfortable journey; the road was cut straight through a monotonous country, and the conveyance was terribly overcrowded. One of the passengers was a heavy-looking priest, and one a peasant woman with a week-old baby she was carrying home to nurse. I put one or two questions to M. le Curé about the Orphan-Idiot Asylums of La Force. Did he know the pastor B—— by name? Had he seen his Orphanages? But M. le Curé, though living in the next parish, seemed alike ignorant of both La Force and its founder. "Pasteur B——, a Protestant? I don't know him at all," he said. We then talked of the little fosterling, asked if it were customary to put out all infants to nurse in La Dordogne. On being answered in the affirmative, we said, "You ought to preach against that, Monsieur le Curé: it is a cruel custom;" and then we questioned the nurse as to the parentage of her little charge. All at once the Curé's face lighted up, and he looked at us as if he were revealing an astounding piece of intelligence.

"Why," he said, "it's the child of Madame

George, my parishioner, and I baptized it myself."

Yet he had never heard of La Force nor of Mettray!

St. Foy is an old-fashioned town, charmingly situated on the banks of the Dordogne. The road to La Force wound along the river side, and had in some places been rendered impassable by the late inundations. As we proceeded on our way, sometimes on foot, sometimes in the crazy old vehicle we had hired, we caught glimpses of scenes so sunny, so full of tender beauty, so poetic, and so peaceful, that we felt as if we would fain escape to La Dordogne whenever the troubles of the world might lie heavy upon us. River, vineyard, hill and wood, all softened and illumined by the autumn sunshine, made up a little rural world very fresh and sweet to live in; one wonders, can any one be very unhappy here?

We brought letters with us from English friends, and the good pastor and his wife received us with more than kindness. Two or three pastors from Geneva were staying in their house, so that

we found ourselves in quite a little Methodist community; and not being Methodists ourselves, though full of respect for all that is good in Methodism, it startled us a little to be catechised thus :—
"The great and good Spurgeon, what is he doing at this moment?" "How many believers are gathered every Sabbath in his temple?" &c. &c. It was so new, too, to feel, in a world where the spirit of inquiry had not yet penetrated, and to know that here, if nowhere else, the authors of *Ecce Homo* and *The Pentateuch Explained* were all but unknown.

Naturally the conversation fell upon the present aspect of Protestantism, or rather Methodism, in France.

"It is very difficult to be a Protestant in France," said Pastor B——, and sighed. "When I think of the reception I had in England, and of the precious friends there whose prayers are ever with me, I compare myself to some solitary exile in a hostile land."

He went on to tell us much that was interesting and unexpected. It seems that the Protestant population decreases in France, on account of the disinclination or disability of the young men to marry, and, in some places, the little communities threaten to die away altogether.

After dinner and coffee, one of the ministers from Geneva gave a little religious discourse, our kindly host extemporised a prayer, and we were conducted to our rooms. But long past midnight we heard earnest voices in discussion, and by daybreak the sounds commenced afresh. It was the Pastor B—— and his friends who sat up late and rose early to discuss the prospects of the Church, as their time of intercourse was drawing to a close. When we came down to breakfast the visitors had gone.

The asylums of La Force are well worth the study of any one interested in the lowest forms of helplessness and suffering. Nothing can equal the cheerfulness and orderliness of the buildings both within and without. The rooms are spacious, well ventilated, and looking on pleasant landscapes of corn-field and vineyard; a pretty church is in construction close by; and both boys and girls have large gardens in which to play or work. The climate of La Dordogne is mild and sunny; snow is almost unknown; and on this November day when we found ourselves at La Force, the temperature was very nearly that of summer. Fortunate, indeed, are these poor idiots who rejoice in such material and moral sunshine; for the loving care and sympathy with which they are surrounded is, I should say, quite unequalled. We have read of the Crimean soldiers kissing Florence Nightingale's shadow as it fell on the wall; and as the good Pastor moved along, there were looks of love and gratitude following him that did the heart good to witness. The most touching feature of Pastor B——'s Orphanages is the way in which the blind are taught to lead the blind. We saw an idiot boy acting as writing-master to a dozen children more or less imbecile, and idiot girls tending upon the paralysed and the epileptic. In one room there were about twenty poor things all more or less personally and mentally deformed; and the distorted faces, bent limbs, oblique eyes, and soulless grins and gesticulations, were horrible. Pastor B—— shuddered at the accustomed sight, and told us that most of these children were born of sin and shame too horrible to mention. With very few exceptions all have been taught to read, to write, to sew, and to labour in the fields; the great hindrance to the good minister's scheme is want of money.

"We have many kind friends and supporters both in England, France, and Switzerland," he said; "and yet we have hard work to pull through. Many people seem to think they do us good service in sending a poor orphan or idiot; we take all in, but at a cost far beyond our present means."

We were glad, and yet sorry, to leave La Force and its generous supporters—glad to escape the sight of so much physical and mental deformity, and sorry that we could not effectually aid the noble efforts made in its behalf.

From La Dordogne to Bayonne extends the dreary desert of the Landes,—a desert only broken by pine-forests and shepherds' huts, and offering no enticement to the impatient travellers bound to Spain. We did, however, spend a day at Arcachon near Bordeaux, for the place had been praised in our hearing as a second and more attractive Biarritz, and we wanted to know how far we might recommend it to friends at home.

I don't think I can recommend any one to go to Arcachon, quiet and pretty as it is. In the first place, the air is so oppressively soft that we both felt stupefied by it, much as if we had taken morphine; and in the second, the houses are all built in such gimcrack style that one feels to be living in a sixpenny peep-show. But, on the other hand, there are sweet-smelling forests of young pine very refreshing to the sight and sense (if people preserve their sight and senses in soporific Arcachon), and salt-baths, and the pleasant feeling that here, if nowhere else in the world, it would be quite possible to become oblivious of every care and responsibility under the sun!

CHAPTER II.

THE MISCONCEPTIONS OF LUGGAGE.—THE COMFORTS OF SPANISH RAILWAY TRAVELLING.—OUR LIBRARY.—FROM THE TROPICS TO THE STEPPES.—GREGORIA AND ISIDORA.—JOURNEY TO MADRID.

"DOS billetes de primera clase para Burgos?" (Two first-class tickets to Burgos) with astonishment repeated the young woman acting as collector at the railway station of Biarritz. "To Burgos! to Burgos!"

"To Burgos," we replied, quietly.

"If you are really going as far as Burgos," she said, with the same look of unmitigated surprise, "I must apply to the station-master for the tickets. Have the goodness to sit down and I will see about it."

We supposed by this young lady's behaviour, and we afterwards found our supposition to be true, that it is a most unusual thing for ladies to travel in Spain. With one or two exceptions, we had the ladies' coupé to ourselves from one end of Spain to the other, and very comfortable travelling we found it.

Our tickets came to hand in due time. We took our seats, the train moved slowly, and we felt fairly off to Spain. There was a pleasant excitement about such a journey just then, for every one prophesied a revolution in Madrid; it might come to-morrow, it must come soon, people said; and we were thought very venturesome to venture beyond the Pyrenees at all. Not that the sense of danger attracted us. We had come to Spain with very definite objects, and though we could not help feeling that the sooner a revolution came for the Spaniards the better, we hoped that it might not come till we were safely at Gibraltar, at least. The pictures of Velasquez, and the Moorish relics of Cordova, Seville, and Granada, were the loadstones that drew us to Spain; at the same time we could not but be alive to the great political and social questions agitating a country once so glorious, and still so capable of glorious things. But in a stay so short as ours was likely to be, we despaired of seeing more than the surface of Spanish thought and life, however much we might wish for other opportunities. It made us smile then, and it makes me smile now, to review the magnitude of our preparations for this trip. And now let me put down, if putting down be possible, a very absurd notion that, to travel comfortably, you should travel without luggage. I have travelled a good deal, and if I were writing a manual for all future tourists, I should affix, as a motto to the book,—"Always travel in your best clothes, and with half-a-dozen trunks at least." Luggage and good clothes take the place of a train of servants. Luggage and good clothes ensure you good places, general civility, and an infinity of minor comforts. Luggage and good clothes will prove your good angels wherever you go. It is all very well for savages to travel without luggage—the Japanese Grandees don't even carry pocket-handkerchiefs about with them; but if any one wants to travel pleasantly and profitably, let him carry a well-stored portmanteau. Surely in no country but patient Spain would two ladies have been allowed to fill the first-class compartment of a railway carriage in the way we did. Under the seats, on the seats, above the seats, were piled an infinite variety of packages, a box of medicines, a folding india-rubber bath, a basket of provisions (a precaution never to be neglected), two or three parcels of books, two or three bundles of rugs, a leather bag of sketching materials, sketching blocks of various sizes, a silk bag of needles and threads; lastly, an odd bag, containing note-books, opera-glasses, passports, a tea-pot, a water-bottle, an etna, an air-cushion, slippers, and sundries without number.

And everything was so useful in its turn. In that long, slow railway journey through Spain, we were, as I have said, always alone. We breakfasted, we dined, we wrote letters and diaries, we read all our books from beginning to end, and we mended our clothes, we made sketches, we made tea, we might have refreshed ourselves with a cold bath, but for want of water. Not a bit of our precious luggage could we have spared, and not a bit ever troubled us beyond the necessity of giving a few cuartos to the porters when changing carriages. As for books we were not half way through Spain before they were done, and yet we had taken a goodly supply; Ford's *Guide,* Street's *Gothic Architecture, Don Quixote* in Spanish, Stirling's *Life of Velasquez,* Washington Irving's pretty twaddle about the Alhambra, Chasles' *Memoir of Cervantes,* the Manuals of Lavice and Viardot, Gautier's book, and half a hundred books about Spain in French, German, English, and Spanish, among others, the delightful and racy sketches of his countrymen, by Don Ramon Mesonero de Romanos.

Of course our luggage accumulated as we went along. We bought books, maps, photographs, clothes everywhere, pottery of Andujar and Talavera, lace from La Mancha, embroidery at Malaga, *capas* at Granada, till, by the time we arrived at our journey's end, our *equipaje,* as the Spaniards call it, was a sight for all beholders.

It was on the tenth of November that we crossed the Pyrenees, all glowing with the purple and gold of autumn, and entered Spain. What a change! It was like coming suddenly from the Tropics to the Steppes. As if by magic, the crimsons, the carnations, the violets, died out of the world, and all became cold and grey and barren. In Old Castile one fancies oneself in a desert— a desert only varied by occasional forests of the *Pinus maritima*, with its straight, weird stem and plumy tuft. The colour and character of the scene varied but slightly—here undulating plains of grey sand piled with columnar masses of granite, there forests of pine, the round bosses of bluish-green standing out sharp and clear against a bright blue sky; or breadths of brown corn-land, lightly ploughed for the autumn seed-sowing. There was something grand and harmonious about this wild monotony—broken rarely by an oasis of a village with ilex groves and yellow acacias and a narrow river winding near, and groups of wide-mouthed Sancho Panzas staring at us as we looked out of the window.

But I must go back to Burgos where the purples and crimsons ended and the desert began. We arrived a little before midnight and felt ourselves at last in Spain. The very air had, as we thought, a foreign smell, and so greatly did this feeling of novelty overcome us that all our Spanish vocabulary seemed to vanish just when it would have stood us in good stead. However, we found places in the omnibus of the Fonda del Norte, and, after waiting about three quarters of an hour, rattled thither in company of several Spanish gentlemen who were wrapped to the chin in their bandit-looking cloaks, and smoked away without intermission. Two or three long-limbed, black-eyed, rosy-cheeked young women, wearing enormous chignons of false hair, but no costume unless untidiness may be called one, led us upstairs flaring candles over our heads. "Dos cuartos," we said; "Si, si," they replied, and on they went, climbing stair after stair, till at last we caught hold of their sleeves in breathless expostulation; and they consented to descend. Finally we were consigned to rooms on the third floor, so spotlessly, ideally clean, that a sanitary inspector could have found nothing to suggest. The rooms had whitewashed walls, iron bedsteads that might have come out of Heal's warehouse, deliciously cool floors of brick-red tiles, wool-mattrasses, sweet-smelling home-spun sheets, and pillows bordered with the lace of La Mancha. We slept delightfully, though the noise of the watchman calling the hours half awoke us now and then.

At seven o'clock, one of the maidens of the chignon, a handsome saucy creature, named Isidora, of whom we grew very fond, brought us chocolate *à l'Espagnol*, namely, tiny cups of sweet, thick chocolate, flavoured with vanilla, rolls of bread, glasses of exquisite water and *azucarillas*, or large crystals of sugar and white of egg. Isidora delighted to give us lessons in Spanish, and went into fits of good-humoured laughter at our blunders. At eleven o'clock we went to the *table d'hôte* breakfast, but there was no one there excepting a Spanish-American family, consisting of a grave father, an insignificant little daughter, and a cosmopolitan son, who spoke a little English. All were very uninteresting, so there was nothing to do but study the dishes, which were all excellent, and *ab ovo usque ad mala*, slightly flavoured with garlic. We had tortillas or omelettes, patties of brains, water-cresses served with oil, olla podrida of bacon, sausage, cabbage, maize cobs, lentils, and other vegetables too numerous to mention, roast snipes, fig jam, and Burgos cheese. The wine was excellent too, but the invariable flavour of tar is not pleasant to the unaccustomed palate. We were served by a waitress handsomer and saucier even than Isidora. She was named Gregoria, and with her napkin swung on her left shoulder went from one to the other, saying her say, and trying to get as much entertainment as was possible out of us. We were very comfortable at Burgos, excepting that it was impossible to keep warm indoors; the sun was shining brilliantly, yet we shivered in our clean bare rooms, which were chimneyless and only warmed by charcoal pans. Round these we squatted like Arabs, but to no purpose, and we went to bed at seven o'clock, finding bed the only warm place. How the cold of winter is endured in Spain I cannot conceive, for winter does come in earnest sometimes, and no preparations seem to be made for it.

We sauntered into the most beautiful old Cathedral on the morning after our arrival, which was Sunday, hoping to find it full of peasants in holiday costume; but though there were plenty of worshippers, except for the sombreros and brown *capas* or cloaks of the men, and the silk and lace mantillas of the women, there was no costume at all. People seem to enjoy going to church in Spain. The ladies come in with their little dogs, drop on their knees on a mat, adjust their fans, and fall into a sort of quiet ecstasy of prayer, the dogs sitting demurely by. The men are equally devout; and every one, caballero or beggar, soldier or priest, comes in his turn, week-day and Sunday. The churches are beautifully kept, warm in cold weather, cool in summer, clean and dusky and quiet always. No wonder they are never empty.

The Cathedral of Burgos is so rich in different sorts of beauty that it would be idle for me to try and particularise any, excepting perhaps the wonderful effect of it as a whole upon the accustomed eye. At first one is quite unable to take in the wonderful simplicity, and strength, and finish of the building, or rather mass of buildings, for it is a city in itself; but later you feel, as it were, a child of the place, loving and living in every part. The colour of the outside is of a soft deep grey, and is unspeakably rich when seen, as we saw it, against quite an Eastern sky. We never grew tired of wandering about the Cathedral, with Street's *Gothic Architecture* in hand to help us through its history; and no one seemed to take offence at us for pursuing such studies within the sacred walls.

I have called the building a city in itself, and if a census were made of its silent population, there might seem some reason in such a simile. Who can doubt that these sculptured saints, archangels, kings, apostles, and monks without, these bleeding Christs, Virgins, infants, and martyrs within, would equal in number the living, moving world of Burgos? And this multitude, stony, silent, dead, though it seems, is not without a power and force that stand in good stead of vitality. Every Christ has its special congregation, every martyr its believers, every saint its legend quickening thousands of devotees to this day.

There is no trace of Moorish influence in the building, and despite many excrescences of bastard-Gothic and Renaissance work, the old Cathedral is still to be seen in all its beauty, reminding you of the purest thirteenth-century Gothic of France. All who have time to study it thoroughly will at the same time acquire a good deal of history, for there is hardly a portion of it which does not show the thought and work of many minds and periods. Spaniard, Gascon, Fleming, Englishman, Florentine, have all had a hand in this glorious work, which gradually increased in size and splendour, till nothing more remained to do except to disfigure it in these later times; which I am sorry to say has been done, within and without, by various means called "restoration."

The ecclesiologist will find plenty to admire at Burgos, but the ordinary traveller will content himself with seeing the Cathedral and the Convents of Miraflores and Las Huelgas. The latter is especially interesting on account of its history. It was founded by the husband of Alienor, daughter of our King Henry II., whose daughter Costanza became abbess. Here numbers of royal ladies took the veil; here kings were crowned and buried; and here a lady abbess still lives and rules, though no longer, as in former days, a princess palatinate, receiving princely revenues.

But what makes Las Huelgas of peculiar value to students is the evidence of Angevine influence in the architecture. Queen Alienor, as Mr. Street justly observes, would naturally procure the help of some architect from her father's dominion of Anjou in the abbey she induced him to found; and one finds here the early vaulting common to old churches in Anjou and Poitou. But these special objects of interest are less interesting than the general effect of the whole place.

It was here, indeed, that we were bodily as well as spiritually transported back to the middle ages. The transformation happened in this wise. After wandering about the cloisters we came unexpectedly upon a scene that simply enchanted us. It was the nuns' chapel. Looking through a screen of delicately wrought cast-iron, we saw two kneeling figures dressed in the black and cream-coloured robes of the Cistercian sisterhood. They were as motionless as statues; and we felt them to be a part of the place as much as the Gothic arches, the stained walls, and the marble altars. So mediæval and ideal was the picture, that, when we came away, we felt as if we of the nineteenth century were dreaming, and the life of those women kneeling in the coloured light the only reality after all!

The roads are so bad around Burgos that it

was with great ado we got to the celebrated Monastery of Miraflores, though it only lies two miles off the town. It is a dreary drive. The road winds around hills so bleak and desolate, as to give us an uneasy suspicion when a beggar in a long black cloak came to the carriage-door begging. He looked exactly like a bandit; and if it had not been for our sturdy coachman we should have trembled for the gold Isabelinoes we carried in our pockets.

Coming home we saw a regiment at practice. The soldiers were the shabbiest set I ever saw, the music poor, and the whole thing spiritless enough; but all the people of Burgos seemed to have turned out for the sight.

In Spain the railways are not made for travellers, but travellers for railways. The trains run so slowly and so seldom that a journey of any length always requires self-denial in the matter of sleep. No matter whither you are bound, to Alicant, to Cordova, to Saragossa, to Badajoz, you must rise early and not go to bed at all; and it is with very great management and disregard of comfort that one can contrive to travel by daylight through the most interesting tracts of scenery.

To go to Madrid in the daytime we had to rise at four o'clock. It is true that the train did not start till nearly seven; but, whether you like it or not, in Spain you are always aroused an hour before you want to get up,—always carried off to the station an hour before the train starts, and to the steamers at least a quarter of a day too soon. People seem in such terrible haste to be rid of you, agreeable as the acquaintance may seem to have been on both sides.

This waiting about in the raw, cold air of an autumn morning is not without its compensations. Everything takes a supernatural shape in the ghastly lamplight; the horses that have brought us here seem, on a sudden, slim and spectral; the long lines of railway carriages have a funereal look; the men, waiting about in their long black cloaks, become brigand-like and terrible to look at; one's own shadow is mysteriously long and dark; one's own voice sounds hollow and unearthly. It is like reading a scene from Mrs. Radcliffe's novels. But when once the train moves slowly off, and the blessed sun warms you, it is the very poetry of railway-travelling. The carriage is so comfortable, the speed so easy, the quiet so delicious, that it is worth while coming to Spain to gain such an experience. No one seems impatient to arrive anywhere; if indeed, any one is bound anywhere. The train stops at every station, and at some so long that you might take photographs in the interval. If you alight to lunch or stretch your limbs a little, you are never hurried back into your carriage, but can loiter about in the pleasant assurance that the train is sure to wait for you. "The train is going to stop; now for a sketch," we used to say when we approached a station; and there was always time.

And then there is the ineffable sense of safety. A single gauge leads from the French frontier to the Spanish capital; the up-train waits for the down train half-way, and each goes its destination as lazily as Kentish farmers jogging to market. How can there be accidents or discomforts under such circumstances?

Tourists are apt to complain of the incivility of officials in Spain. I can only say that we travelled from Biarritz to Gibraltar, and encountered nothing but courtesy and kindness. We spoke a little

Spanish, it is true, and had left England with a solemn compact never to get out of temper, which may, perhaps, in some degree account for such experience. And we always travelled in the first-class carriage reserved for ladies. I do not think English ladies would find second and third-class travelling pleasant, on account of the smoking.

Thus we travelled through the brown deserts of Old Castille to Madrid. Treeless, tawny, and interminable, anything more dreary than these same Spanish steppes cannot well be conceived. Yet there was contrast and colour for the artistic eye. There was mass after mass of cool, grey limestone against a bright blue sky; and when the sun set over the undulating table-lands, a weird, fiery, unimagined splendour not to be put into any words!

CHAPTER III.

THE GAIETY OF MADRID.—THE IMPERATIVENESS OF TEETOTALISM THERE.—THE QUEEN AND THE ROYAL BIRTHDAY.—ROADS AND RIVER-BANKS.—APROPOS OF BULLS.

THERE is no more stir at the railway-station of Madrid than at that of Tunbridge Wells or Chelmsford; and as you rattle along the quiet streets, you ask yourself—Can this be the capital of so many great kingdoms? It is the fashion to represent Madrid as a dreary place, but, on the contrary, its first aspect is eminently cheerful. The streets are light and airy, the sky is generally without a cloud, and the population is a gay and unique one. I suppose Madrid is the only capital in Europe where the upper classes can be said to cling to anything like costume, for certainly the long cloaks of the men, and the mantillas and fans of the ladies, do merit the name of costume still. In Spain it is possible for a man to be dainty about his dress, since every cloak can be lined in different styles of luxury, with silk, with velvet, with fur, or with brocade. The upper cape of the cloak is thrown over the left shoulder in such a manner as to expose the lining; and as you walk along the streets, you are lost in admiration of a dress so graceful, and think regretfully of the orthodox great-coat worn in London, when a little colour would be so pleasant to the eye. Put a Spanish cloak upon every man in Fleet Street and Piccadilly, and how the bits of creamy fur, of crimson silk, of purple velvet, of gold brocade, would enliven these sober thoroughfares! But the Madrilenians are not a majestic race, though so majestically equipped. Diminutive in size, sallow, shaven like monks, one never dreams of calling the men handsome. At the same time they have, for the most part, beautiful features and fine eyes. The ladies, tripping about fan in hand, are pretty; but, like the men, frail-looking and without dignity. Treacherous as is the climate, they go about bare-necked, bare-headed, and with only a fan to shade them from a dangerous sun. Yet one sees the same thing everywhere—whilst the women wear tight-fitting clothes, and expose themselves to wind and sun, the men are wrapped up like Arabs in the easiest, most sensible dress possible. In England we are growing wiser, and we no longer kill our young girls by making them wear tight stays, thin shoes, and back-boards; but in Madrid—I suppose one of the unhealthiest places in the world—it never seems to enter into any one's head that what is dangerous to a man is doubly so to a woman.

It will be easily understood why Madrid should be so unhealthy when a little consideration is given to its site. Built on a plateau 2412 feet above the sea, it is exposed to an African sun and a Siberian winter. Like Rome it stands in a treeless desert; and the icy winds may blow down from the chain of the Guadarrama, whilst the sun is scorching with fiery powers. You may pass in a moment from a cold climate to a hot one in Madrid; and at all times the air is so rarefied as to be terribly trying. I enjoy excellent health as a rule, but the climate of Madrid knocked me down in a day. I was tormented by a constant neuralgia; my face swelled up so that I could hardly see out of my eyes; and I became so languid that I could hardly set one foot before the other. Yet one must not take stimulants. Never shall I forget the dismay with which an English lady saw me take wine at dinner.

"Unless you are mad," she said, "you will drink no wine here. When I first came to Madrid I felt as you do, feverish, listless, utterly good for nothing, and I tried a little *vin ordinaire* as a remedy, but it acted like a poison. My face became covered with a terrible eruption, and if I had not abstained in time, I should have had the *colico* of Madrid. It is a terrible climate alike for body and mind, and thankful enough shall I be to get away."

Every one coughs everywhere. The men cover their mouths and keep on the sunny side of the street, as if death lurked in a "shady place;" whilst the ladies (would to heaven they did cover their mouths when the icy wind blows from the mountains!), who go bareheaded, have a frightfully fragile look. Indeed it is the very rarest thing to see a really robust-looking person in Madrid.

The curled darlings of society are pale as spectres, the waiters and shopmen are thin and cadaverous; a fresh, beautiful look of health one meets nowhere. I don't think this matter of climate is sufficiently taken into account by those who write about Spain and the Spaniards; for there is no denying the fact that since Madrid became the capital of this great country, its greatness grew pale and wan. Bred in a hot-bed of consumption, of colic, and all sorts of diseases, is it any wonder that the Madrilenian degenerates both in body and in mind, till he no longer looks capable either of mental or physical exertion? Wherever we found ourselves, at the Prado, at a review, on the Puerto de Sol, or in the churches, we were always looking at the sickly, lethargic population around us, with the thought—Is this the stuff of which reformations and revolutions are to be made?

And then the dire effects of the Inquisition must be taken into account. Who can doubt that for some of the mental and physical debasement witnessed in Spain at the present day the system of Ignatius Loyola is alone responsible? Torture, enslave, terrify a dozen men and women, and see what their children and children's children will become? But whether this reasoning may be received as a mere fancy or not, the fact remains incontestable,—the upper ten thousand of Madrilenian population is the most miserable-looking of any in the world. Of Madrilenian society we had no experience, for, though we were furnished with letters of introduction, more important objects claimed our time. It is the greatest mistake to do two things at once, and having come to Madrid to see and study the Velasquez Gallery, we had no inclination to neglect this end for any other. As a substitute for personal experience, we read Spanish newspapers, modern Spanish novels, and plays; and though, as far as the latter goes, it was rather hard work, we felt the curriculum to be instructive. Putting aside the charming stories of Caballero and Trueba, the modern Spanish novel is a poor affair, and the play a poor affair too; but any one who really wishes to be entertained and instructed should read the social sketches of such writers as Don Ramon Mesonero de Romanos, Pedro de Medrazo, and José de Larra, who describe their country and countrymen with inimitable grace, satire, and discrimination.

And the newspapers, what is to be said of them? I think this paragraph might be headed,— "There are no newspapers in Spain;" for except as mediums of advertisements and local gossip, they don't exist. On first installing ourselves in the comfortable Hôtel de Paris, we used to fly eagerly to the reading-room, laying hands on *La Correspondencia de España*, *La Gaceta*, *La Regeneracion*, &c., &c.; but very little did they tell us excepting the small-beer chronicles of every nation under the sun, and of Spain above all. Then there would be *feuilletons* of very inferior quality, long lists of advertisements for wet-nurses, and invitations to the friends of the late Don or Doña So-and-so to attend his or her funeral obsequies.

Of anything like political news, much less political discussion, there was seldom a vestige.

But though the Government has succeeded in bridling the tongue of the press, there is abundance of contraband talk in Madrid. No matter with whom you converse, the topic is sure to be of bloody revolutions and retributions unequalled in history. But mention the Royal name, and, whether you are among aristocrats or peasants, you will see dark looks, meaning shrugs of the shoulder, gestures significant of bitterest meaning.

"It must come soon," people say to you; "and the sooner the better, though dire will be the coming of it. Never in history were such wrongs, such hatred, such tyranny, to be washed out in blood. We can only watch and wait."

The acquaintance of a day,—nay, of an hour, is sufficient to warrant all sorts of confidences on public matters from a Spaniard, and this incautiousness, or rather candour, makes you forgive even his love of the bull-fight. It is, indeed, a most consolatory fact, that it is but a watching and waiting in Spain, and that underneath a semblance of indifference burns and rages a wholesome desire of liberty.

"We are at the present moment enduring a tyranny of which foreigners have no conception," said a cultivated Spaniard to me, one day, in English; "and yet, despite of all that is going on secretly among us, no one can say when things will change. Change they must; we shall have the French Revolution acted over again in the streets of Madrid." *

Again: we were taken to see the graves of

* There are very able and interesting articles on the condition and prospects of Spain in Mr. Grant Duff's admirable *Studies in European Politics*, in the *Revue des Deux Mondes* for September 1865, and in *Fraser's Magazine* for December 1865. I quote one closing passage from the writer in the *Revue*, M. Charles Mazade:—" L'Espagne est dans un de ces états presque indéfinissables : à la veille encore on dit qu'une révolution est impossible, parcequ'on n'aperçoit pas un but précis, et au lendemain, lorsqu'elle a éclaté, on se demande comment elle n'est pas arrivée plus tot, parceque tout le monde y travaillait. Je ne veux point dire assurément que cet état si grave qu'il paraisse lorsque ces crises deviennent plus aigues, que cet état soit sans remède. L'Espagne possède, sans doute, en elle-même les élémens d'un développement de fortune matérielle, comme elle a enfin tous les éléments d'une puissance extérieure proportionnée à sa situation, à ses interêts, et à ses ambitions légitimes ; mais ce qui est vrai aussi, c'est que les hommes, les partis, ont à secouer bien des préjugés, bien des illusions, bien des passions, dont la trace est visible dans la politique contemporaine, et qui ne sont point étrangères aux crises actuelles. Ils ont à se pénétrer, tout d'abord, de cette vérité d'où découlent toutes les autres, qui éclatent dans l'histoire la plus récente,—que tout ce que favorise l'absolutisme accelère la décomposition de la péril, qu'une politique libérale n'eut pas même seulement une condition de progrès, qu'elle est plus encore peut-être aujourd'hui, une stricte garantie d'ordre et de préservation."

some young officers of high family who were shot in prison during the disturbances of last year. A respectable man of the lower ranks was standing near, and he said, with tears in his eyes, but half-suppressed curses on his lips,—

"They were as innocent as new-born babes; though, thank God! this murder won't long want vengeance."

It would be almost impossible to convey any idea of the bitterness and hatred we found underlying the public mind at this epoch.

People gave us their confidences without any reason for doing so, confidences which all amounted to one and the same thing—contempt of the tyranny and resolutions to overturn the tyrants. "No one can tell how uncomfortable it is to live in Madrid now," said an English lady to me one day. "It is the old fable of the sheep and the wolves over and over again. We are constantly laying in stores for three or four weeks' siege; but I've done it so often in vain that I have determined never to do it again, and I daresay the consequence will be that a revolution will come and find my larder empty."

And yet how gay it was in Madrid! Though the north-east wind blew from the mountains, ladies promenaded the streets bareheaded; and Opera-house, Plaza de Toros, Prado, and every other haunt of amusement, was crowded. We naturally tried each in turn. We saw a review on the Queen's birthday, went to the Opera, drove on the Prado, and, much against my inclination, I spent twenty minutes at a bull-fight. The review was a spiritless affair, every one had prophesied some sort of outbreak on that day, but none came; and the Queen, who had been hissed at the theatre a few days before, did not appear. The King took her place, and very flushed and uncomfortable he looked. Not so le Père Claret, the Queen's confessor. As he descended the palace steps to his handsome carriage drawn by four splendid mules, he looked quite contented with the existing order of things,—which I suppose is but natural,—and stepped along in his purple robes with as much dignity as if he had been the Pope himself. This man's history and position are so extraordinary that one cannot but look after him with interest. By turns, soldier, ecclesiastic, missionary, and bishop, he has won a certain celebrity for his sermons and the publication of a coarse book called *La Clave de Oro*, and he has also won the royal ear. His rival in this latter respect is a nun, called Maria-Dolorès Patrocinio, abbess of the convent of St. Pascual d'Aranjuez, who was tried and condemned some time since by the tribunal, because she gave herself out to be the subject of a miracle, pretending to have the wounds of Christ on her hands. One can but pity the Queen, who has laid herself open to such unmitigated obloquy by her favouritism. No young sovereign ever passed through stormier ordeals than Isabella the Second. Pity that experience has not taught her wisdom, and that by her own hand she has undone, Penelope-wise, good deeds done in the gentleness of youth! There is a little book called *The Attaché in Madrid*, which gives some highly interesting sketches of the Spanish Court and capital during the eventful July of 1854. It was a reign of terror, and the Queen was as a shuttlecock driven hither and thither; but a Spanish mob is not a French mob, and always showed some threadbare kind of respect for royalty. An English writer on the affairs of Spain, says, " The Queen of

Spain is not unpopular with the bulk of her subjects" (which statement I doubt), "and her great failing is, that feminine one to which Dr. Reaumur attributes all Mary Queen of Scots' errors, '*Sie konnte nicht ohne Männer leben.*'" But it seems to me that it is faults of both heart and head that have made the throne of Isabella the Second the bed of thorns it is. If, despite a bad government, Spain is making undeniable progress, who can doubt what she might be under a good? I think no one who has had opportunity of studying her domestic history during the last thirty years will be inclined to agree with Mr. Buckle's sweeping assertions. He despaired of the regeneration of Spain, but slow though the process must be, it has undoubtedly commenced. In commerce, in education, in literature, it has commenced; and who shall stem the flow of that slow but inevitable tide?

The great hindrance is from the badness and uncertainty of the government. There is no security in the land, without which there can be no spirit of enterprise. Who can say what to-morrow will bring forth? "A Spanish cabinet," an English writer wittily says, "may be compared to a Chili house, constructed on a calculation that an earthquake will occur within the year." All the best energy of the nation is spent upon the unhealthy excitement of political transformations. It is like living in an atmosphere overcharged with electricity. One moment, there is a succession of lightning-flashes, all sorts of brilliant miraculous heralds of a tempest that is to clear the air; then comes a growl of thunder, an outburst of popular feeling in Barcelona or some distant part; and all is hushed again for a short space, when the symptoms occur again and again without coming to a crisis.

But this underlying suspense and unrest do not interfere with the gay, out-of-door life of Madrid. The weather is always fine, and the Prado is always crowded.

There is nothing livelier in Europe than this same Prado, with its crowd of pretty ladies, picturesque cavaliers, dear little carriages for babies drawn by spotlessly white lambs, nurses from Estramadura in short, brown petticoats, embroidered with gold, water-sellers in sombrero and leathern gaiters, and an infinity of equipages, costumes, and cries, to distract the eye and ear of the foreigner. But if you are tired of gaiety, in ten minutes you can get into a scene so peaceful and quiet, that you might fancy yourself miles away from a capital. Drive down to the green banks of the Manzanares, where a thousand peasant women are beating linen in the afternoon sun. Their red and yellow skirts, and plentiful black hair, make quite a picture, and their blithe talk and singing never cease for a moment. Yet how tranquil and rustic it is here! One has a superb view of Madrid, with its background of blue and white mountains, palace and church and house-top flushing in the light of the setting sun, whilst the hum of its busy life seems silenced for a while. The river winds amid sloping banks of lustrous green, lightly sprinkled with yellow foliage, and team after team winds its sleepy way towards some village seen in the distance.

It sounds incredible, and yet it is true, that, within half-an-hour's drive of Madrid, the roads are impracticabilities for any carriage having springs. I do not think there is a lane in Sussex, or in any heavy land district of Suffolk, where you could be so jolted in a tumbril as we were in a light cab just outside the Spanish capital. We found the same state of things throughout our journey. I suppose there is no functionary answering to that of our parish surveyor. No one seems to mind having his bones rattled over the stones, as if he were a "pauper whom nobody owns."

I feel in duty bound to say a word about the Bull-fight, though let no one shut this book, thinking that I am about to describe that horror of horrors. Heaven knows, it is a sight that any one might make something of, for added to the accessories of a burning blue sky, and a picturesque assemblage of nine thousand people excited to the verge of frenzy, there are all the savage elements of the human and animal nature called into full play. But what I saw of "this bloody amphitheatre of Rome, with spectators in hats and coats," as Ford calls it, so sickened me, that I never recur to the subject without repugnance. Before I left England I was told by an educated Spaniard that bull-fights were going out of fashion, and that his countrymen, at least those of the upper classes, no longer attended them. But what did personal experience teach me? It taught that Spanish ladies do go to bull-fights, and, moreover, that they take with them their young children, who clap their hands at the close of every bloody act, and watch the whole cruel drama as eagerly as their elders.

To judge fairly of those horrid amusements, you should go behind the scenes. There, in a dreary chapel, you see the *matadors*, the *banderilleros*, and all the other wretched actors in the play, taken by turns to confess and receive absolution at the hands of a priest. How ghastly pale and craven they look in their tinselly dresses!—more like culprits going to execution than the proud heroes of great feats. Adjoining the chapel is a room fitted up as a hospital, which is too often called into requisition; and from this you are led to the stables, where stand wretched hacks, soon to be blindfolded and tortured to death. These poor animals, it is said,—let us hope without truth,—are often the discarded and superannuated favourites of gentlemen; but no matter what they may have been, they are brought on the stage to be gored by turns, and their blood and agony count for nothing.

The arena is by no means imposing till it is filled with spectators; and the procession is tawdry enough. The dogs and mules which figure in it, are alone worth looking at. The former are called into requisition to madden any bull that does not show game, the latter to drag away the dead horses and bulls. But as soon as the horrid play begins, the place becomes a very *infernus*. Men and women vie with each other in noises, screams, and cries; now it is some unfortunate *chulo* who is the butt of the whole assembly, because he has allowed the bull to attack the horse too soon; now it is a *picador*, who gets praised by shouts, clappings of the hand, and all sorts of uproarious applause; and now it is the bull who becomes the pet of the moment for having skilfully overturned horse and rider. If anything can be more unbearable than the spectacle itself, it is the behaviour of the spectators. The noise is deafening,—nay, maddening; and when the first act of the drama ended, we rushed away too horrified to put our horror into words.

The wide street leading to the Plaza de Toros was so crowded with people going to the bull-fight, that it was with some difficulty we could get along. All Madrid seemed turning out for the sight, and yet it was a weekly one; and, on this occasion, of no exceptional attractiveness. On grand festivals there are extra bulls killed and far greater crowds; but all who wish to know more about bull-fights, past and present, should go to that fountain-head of knowledge on Spanish affairs, Richard Ford.* There is one consideration apt to be overlooked by those who are studying the subject, and that is, the hand-to-hand struggle between man and brute. From the moment the show com-

* Of all amusing writers on Spain, commend me to Richard Ford and George Borrow. What a fantastic world they lived in, and how much they contrived to see where other people would have beheld blank space and " nothing more." Ford's opinions, and I should say Borrow's stories, must both be swallowed with a grain of salt; with the exception, perhaps, of what the former says about bull-fights. See the *Quarterly Review*, No. cxxiv., *The Handbook*, and *The Gatherings*.

mences till its close every player, whether he be chulo or banderillero, picador or matador, places his life in peril—not for the love of sport, mind, but for the sake of gain—and frequent occurrence of grave accidents, and the possibility of fatal ones, may well account for the pale faces of these desperate creatures. Only a few weeks before our arrival at Madrid, a well-known matador had been killed at Seville, and the whole horrid scene was described to us by an eye-witness. There was no show of sympathy made for the man; but cries of "Brava, toro! Bravo, toro!" filled the arena from end to end. The son of the murdered man took his father's place!

For my part all my sympathies go with the bull. He, poor beast! is often the most peace-loving creature in the world, and, anyhow, suffers ten times more than the horse, which is not goaded into frenzy by shouts, arrows, fire-works, sword-pricks, and dogs, but is allowed to die quickly. The bull is tortured to the last as if he were a heretic. Pitiful it is to see him crawl into some quiet corner to die, with

The Uses of Bull-fights. 61

what regrets for his peaceful pastures, with what horror of his tormentors, with what quivering agony in every nerve, Heaven alone knows!

It sounds incomprehensible, and yet it is quite true, that bull-fights are often held for charitable purposes. A few years back a new church at Madrid was to be built. A committee was formed for the purpose, consisting of an archbishop, several bishops, noblemen, and others; the land was given, and the building commenced. But some money was wanting, and so they had a bull-fight, the proceeds of which helped them on a little. Later, their necessities were even more pressing, and they tried another bull-fight. This time, however, the owner of the bull-ring refused to give them a benefit, and other means had to be tried.

Cruelty begets cruelty, and as if the appetite for blood were not satisfied at the circus, the churches offer more in abundance. Anything more revolting than the bleeding, bruised Christs and saints, cannot be conceived. No shape nor symbol of suffering is left out of the dreary catalogue till one comes away, sick with the ghastly blasphemies witnessed on every side. This is all the sadder, since a real spirit of religious fervour seems predominant; and the brighter side of Romanism is never wholly hidden from the eyes of even the most superficial or prejudiced observer.

And what has not Murillo done to beautify this Church of Spain, whose annals are so stained with blood and tears?

CHAPTER IV.

VELASQUEZ, THE PAINTER OF MEN.—MURILLO, THE PAINTER OF ANGELS.—RIBERA, THE PAINTER OF INQUISITORS.—ZURBARAN, THE PAINTER OF MONKS.—GOZA, THE HOFFMAN OF SPANISH ART.—THE QUIETUDE OF THE GALLERIES.

WE had come ostensibly to Madrid to see the works of Velasquez, and we carried out our intention, not glancing at, but really looking into and studying them as we study Homer, or Shakespeare, or Cervantes. The journey from London to Madrid is costly and fatiguing; but I advise any one to make it who is desirous of receiving a good lesson in art. I own that no one has taught me such a lesson on the largeness of it, the perfectibility of it, the ease of it. Velasquez' work is simple creation, and that is the truth of it. Where will you find work like it? He was no poet like Murillo or Raphael. He sucked in no golden atmosphere that saints and seraphs breathe; he heard no music of the upper spheres, but he lived among ordinary men and women, and portrayed them, flesh and spirit, without an extravagance, without an idealism, without the hairbreadth of a deviation from the truth. Thus it happens that when you come away from his pictures, you forget the painter and the painting, and you remember only the subjects,—not elevated subjects, often quite the contrary, but æsthetically conceived by an intellect so unswerving, and touched with a hand so masterly, that they seem to "live, and move, and have their being."

As has been truly said, "He drew the minds of men; they live, breathe, and seem ready to walk out of their frames. The dead come forth conjured up; we behold what written history cannot give—their actual semblance in life. His power of painting circumambient air, his knowledge of lineal and aërial perspective, the gradation of tones in light, and shadow, and colour, give an absolute concavity to the flat surface of his canvas; we look into space, into a room, into the reflexion of a mirror." And elsewhere, "Aucun maître ne saisit comme lui un personnage pour le faire vivre, agir, respirer devant vous. En même temps, quelle tournure il lui donne ! Comme il a le secret de cette fleur d'insolence et de ces belles rodomontades, dont à nos yeux l'hidalgo Castilien est le type !"

I suppose most people would prefer Murillo to Velasquez, because imagination is generally set on a pedestal above intellect. Murillo's imagination is like an upsoaring fountain, ever sunny and ever luminous, whilst Velasquez did not dream, but reason. He is, indeed, the most logical of painters ; and what makes his works so valuable to artists and lovers of art is the quality they have in common with the masterpieces of antiquity, and which has been well called the perfection of good sense. As a French author has said, " Velasquez écrit en prose, mais, pour le portrait, du moins, il est le premier des prosateurs."

The Museo of Madrid contains more than sixty pictures of this great master,—the Voltaire of art, who tried his hand at everything and succeeded in everything,—portraits, landscapes, historic subjects, animals, interiors, flowers, fruit. There is nothing he left untried excepting the marine. It is quite astounding with what nobility he treated ignoble subjects, such as dwarfs, beggars, dull Infantas, and kings with " the foolish hanging of the nether lip," painting all to the life; for though Velasquez was a courtier and a court-painter, he never flattered his royal patrons one iota. He treated ignoble subjects nobly, that is, faithfully, seeing and respecting in dwarfs, beggars, and foolish Infantas and kings, the same humanity that he saw in such lofty, stately Spaniards as he has elsewhere given.

Study one of Velasquez' greatest pictures as a whole, as a creation in fact, and then set yourself to look into the manner of it, how much remains still to marvel at and admire. Moratin said, " Velasquez knew how to paint the air;" and nothing is more striking in his pictures than this clear, palpable, sunny atmosphere ; one seems to breathe in it, and not in that of the galleries.

But when you have made this discovery, you will make others no less striking. Take, for instance, his colouring. Perhaps no painter ever employed fewer colours than he; he is as sparing of bright tints as a classic writer in the use of similes, yet his pictures glow with life and are perfect miracles of harmony and truth to nature. His painting has been well compared to a stately gentleman who maintains in his conduct, his actions and his words, a perfect and dignified equilibrium, and who avoids loud laughter or talking, or anything that might disturb the general harmony of his bearing and appearance.

His work, indeed, resembles his life, which was courtly, dignified, and complete. Though a courtier, he kept intact his pure manners and morals, his kindly nature, and his passionate love of art. All that is known of him redounds to his honour, from the period of his early youth, when he worked in the studio of Pacheco, and by his fine qualities of heart and brain won his master's affection and the hand of his master's daughter, to the fatal journey to Irun in 1660, where he brought on his death by overworking himself in preparing the 'Ile de Faisans' for the Infanta's marriage. Of all noble Spaniards, hardly Cervantes seems to have been nobler than he.

It were worth any one's while to make the

journey to Madrid, if only to see his *Borrachos*; and there is a good story about our English Wilkie, who came to Madrid for the purpose of studying Velasquez, and went away having studied this one masterpiece only.

Wilkie used to visit the gallery every day, no matter what the weather might be, and to establish himself in a chair opposite this picture. After having contemplated it fixedly for three hours in silent ecstasy, he would utter a long and profound "ouf," seize his hat, and rush away.

Hanging close (if I remember rightly) to the wonderful "Las Meninias," is a religious picture, which every one should look at, for never had picture a stranger and more touching history.

Don Diego Rodriguez de Silva y Velasquez, the rich courtier, the familiar friend of the king, and the renowned artist, had a mulatto slave named Juan Pareja. It was Pareja's office to mix the colours, to prepare the canvas, to clean the brushes, to arrange the palettes; and these occupations kept him perpetually in his master's studio. He felt himself to be a born painter all the time that he exercised these humble duties, he watched his master at work, he listened to the instruction he gave his pupils, he spent his nights in making sketches and copies secretly. At last, when he was forty-five years old, he thought himself sufficiently accomplished in his art to make his secret known. Accordingly, one day he placed a small picture of his own, with its face turned to the wall, among his master's; and when the king came to the studio, as he often did, brought it forward. "That's a beautiful picture," said Philip; "whose work is it?" Upon which Pareja threw himself on his knees and avowed that it was his own. Velasquez freed him from slavery by a public act, and received him, from that day, among his pupils and equals. But poor Pareja was so used to service and so devoted to his master, that he would fain have served him as a freedman; and after the great painter's death continued so to serve his daughter.

From Velasquez, who lived in an age when Spain was great, and interpreted the spirit of it with the faithfulness of photography, and an introspective power quite Shakspearian, one naturally turns to his friend and pupil, the divine Murillo.

At first sight, the blazing sun of Velasquez'

genius would seem to obscure and dwarf the paler orb of Murillo's. It is like passing from Cervantes to Calderon; and if the one paints men and manners with inimitable force and humours, the other takes us straight up to heaven, where we abide with saints and angels.

It is curious that the distinctive recognition of Murillo as a great religious painter should not yet have generally taken place in England. People who do not travel and read Mr. Ruskin's criticisms, think of Murillo only or chiefly as a painter of dirty and vicious humanity, such as beggar boys and the like. Yet how unlike is such an impression, and how easy it is to know what Murillo really has done, even without going to Spain! There is one picture alone, in the possession of Mr. Tomline,* of Orwell Park, Ipswich, which tells you more about Murillo than anything English critics ever wrote. I did not see this picture till after I returned from

---

* To see this and Mr. Tomline's other fine pictures, it is necessary to write for permission, which is most willingly granted. Without such a precaution, you are like the foolish virgins unprovided with oil, and have to go away in despair. The pretty scenery around may prove a little consolation.

Spain, though I had endeavoured to do so (having ridden eighteen miles for the purpose), but other travellers will be wise to see everything they can, not only of Murillo, but of Velasquez and other Spanish masters, before starting for tawny Spain. Some of Murillo's finest pictures are at Seville, but as the Gallery of Madrid contains forty-five of his works, it is not necessary to go to Seville to see what this man of such rare gifts could do.

Murillo's life was very different to that of Velasquez; and if his works are unequal,—some being inferior both in conception and finish—it must be remembered that he was no favoured friend of royalty, working at his leisure, and never hurried into laboured or crude execution by the necessity of money. Murillo painted for the public and for his bread; and whilst some of his works are glorious achievements of fancy and skill, full-blown blossoms of beauty that have ripened in the sun, others have evidently been too hastily conceived and matured. A French author, who has written discriminately about Murillo, draws an admirable distinction between his works and those of Velasquez, Titian, or Da Vinci, when he says that a *chef d'œuvre* of Murillo is only a *chef d'œuvre* relatively, and by comparison, whilst a *chef d'œuvre* of the latter painter's is a *chef d'œuvre* absolute, defying all comparison whatever. He says, and very truly, that the possessor of one canvas of Murillo, were it the most beautiful of all, would have but a very incomplete idea of this painter, whilst a single masterpiece of Raphael or Titian suffices to attest their genius to the full.*

But setting aside criticisms and comparisons, what a legacy of beauty has Murillo left the world! With what deep religious fervour and poetic feeling he has embodied all that was most divine in the Catholic religion! There is not a phase of heavenly contemplation, or fervid ecstasy, that he has not made incarnate and immortal in enchanted colours; and if you contemplate his pictures for awhile, you seem to drop your fleshly garments and float in golden ether with rapt virgins and smiling cherubs. His colour has well been called ravishing; it is something impossible to describe, and as much the soul of the picture as essence is the soul of the flower.

* Revue des Deux Mondes, July 1861. Du Goût Contemporaine.

This colouring is so delicious that it is no less of a vision to seeing eyes than miraculous healing would be to the blind man. I ought, perhaps, to say to Northern eyes, since Murillo's atmospheres are hardly less luminous and lovely than those of his native Andalusia. He painted Andalusian beauty too, like Velasquez preferring to portray real to ideal human nature, though, unlike Velasquez, he contented himself with loveliness only. "One might say," says M. Viardot, "that Velasquez is the painter of earth, and Murillo the painter of heaven." He should have added,—of heaven as peopled by the believing Catholic with beautiful beneficent Christs, with archangels, angels, seraphs, with the noble army of martyrs, with Virgins ever fair and ever young, with crowned saints, and heavenly hosts shining resplendent round celestial thrones.

To understand a great religious painter like Murillo, one must have some sympathy with the age in which he lived, and the public which was his patron. He was eminently the painter of the people, from the time of his unlettered and humble boyhood, when he sold little pictures of Virgins and Christs at a few rials the dozen in the streets of Seville, to the last years of his long, independent, prosperous, honoured life. It must be remembered that the Inquisition kept a strict *surveillance* on artists, their works and their patrons; and that Velasquez is almost an exception in his divergence from the only fair field open to all, an exception impossible perhaps except to a royal favourite. Murillo's more plastic genius accommodated itself to the circumstances surrounding it, and the result is, these marvels of colour and celestial expression, that realize the spirit of the time at once.

Whilst Velasquez may be said to have embodied in his works the aristocratic spirit of the most aristocratic age of Spain, and Murillo the purely devotional, Zurbaran may be called the painter of the ascetic, and Ribera, better known as Spagnoletto, of the Inquisitorial. Amateurs will not, I think, care much for Ribera's pictures, except in so far as they show the cruel side of the same religion that in Murillo's hands was so sweet and lovely. Ribera, or, as he has been called, "this cruel forcible imitator of ordinary ill-selected nature," may be well studied at Madrid. Here you have every form and fashion of suffering and repulsive humanity, such, as Ford said, could be conceived by a bull-fighter, and please a people whose sports are blood and torture; and if for the sake of the powerful in drawing, and the wonderful mastery of light and shadow, you can contemplate those terrible subjects one after the other, you will have more powers of endurance and more passion for art than the present writer. This Spanish Caravaggio, who obtained his name of *lo Spagnoletto*, the little Spaniard, when he was a begging student in the streets of Rome, lived so much in Italy, and had such a passion for the great Italian masters, Correggio and Caravaggio, whom he studied, that, except in Madrid, one hardly thinks of him as a Spaniard at all. His busy and afterwards prosperous life was mostly spent at Naples, then a province of Spain, though the greater part of his pictures have been recovered by his native country; but it was not a life to look into so fearlessly as that of Velasquez or Murillo, and one gladly turns alike from the master and his work to others less painful.

Zurbaran has left no story. Like so many of the

greatest Spanish painters, he arose from the humblest ranks, and that is almost all one knows of him. But he was a very great artist, and his pictures have the same historic interest as those of Murillo, portraying, as they do, a distinct phase of Catholic Spain. Indeed, a French critic has gone so far as to say that if by a miracle the remembrance of Spain were effaced from the universal human mind; and if we were ignorant of her moral and religious history, such pictures as these of Murillo, Zurbaran, Ribera, and Herrera, would lose half their worth. It is quite certain that Zurbaran's pictures do owe much of their interest to the ascetic element prevailing in them, however far we may be from accepting the above conclusion. He saw a monk, and painted a monk introspectively, as no one else could do; and every one will do well to study his pictures, the finest of which are at Seville, and very few of which are at Madrid. They portray the austere element of the same religion which Murillo made so enticing with visions of light, loveliness, and colour. These three masters, Murillo, Ribera, and Zurbaran, may be said to express and eliminate the three vital principles of Romanism, such as men like Loyola and women like St. Theresa had made it, namely, ecstatic vision, torture, and asceticism. It seems as if in Spain the Trinity must stand or fall together.

The schools of Spanish art are generally divided into three, the Castilian, the Valencian, and the Sevillian; properly speaking, the kingdom of Aragon possessed another, though little known. Gallegos, who introduced the style of Van Eyck and Albert Dürer; Moralès, whose Ecce Homos and Madonna Dolorosas are scattered all over Spain; *El Mudo*, the dumb, who brought from Italy something of the rich Venetian colouring; El Greco, who was at once an architect, a sculptor, and a painter, "truly Spanish, unequal and eccentric," and whose " streaky lights," as Mr. Stirling says, " are sharper than Toledo blades;"— may be said to represent the school of Castile; whilst that of Valencia, the most effeminate and superstitious province of Spain, is represented by Ribaeta, the disciple of L. Carracci and Domenichino, and Ribera, Orrente, the Bassano of Spain. Then we come to Seville, the capital of sunny, many-gifted

Andalusia. The school of Seville boasts of other honourable names before we come to its greatest —Velasquez, Murillo, and Zurbaran. There was Herrera, the first master of Velasquez; Pacheco, his second master and afterwards father-in-law, not only a painter of some pretensions, but a learned writer on art,—"coldly correct and classically dull in whatever he did," says a critic; but let that pass. There was Pablo de Cespedes, also famous for achievements of pen and pencil; Juan de las Ruelas, the worthy pupil of Correggio and Giorgione, whose pictures are only to be seen in Andalusia. Alonzo Cano, alike architect, sculptor, and painter, whose passion for art was so strong, that on his dying bed he impatiently put a crucifix from his lips because it was badly carved.

What a splendid muster-roll is this! Who will not be tempted to come and judge for himself? The works of many of these artists, however, are only to be seen in the churches and convents of their native provinces, where they remain "hanging like golden oranges on their native boughs."

But before leaving Madrid, you must give a little time—not too much, since it is so precious—

among "these acres of canvas," to the fantastic and not pleasing pictures of Goya, the last Spanish painter of any note, who died in 1828, at the age of eighty-six. Goya has been compared to Hogarth for his quality of humour; to Callot, for imagination; to Rembrandt, for vigour of execution, elsewhere to Velasquez and to Reynolds; but his pictures are so characterised by a sort of Hoffman-like revelling in the weird and the impossible, that it is difficult to understand and like them. Like Ribera he bids you sup on horrors.

And after this survey of all the Spanish painters, how much remains yet to see! Here are grand pictures of Titian, Tintoretto, Veronese, of Michel-Angelo, Andrea del Sarto, of Domenichino, —indeed, of all the Italian, Flemish, and French masters, and amongst so much to see, the only fear is of seeing nothing.

Our principal object in coming to Madrid was Velasquez, who is to be studied nowhere else, and we therefore saw many other pictures imperfectly. Other travellers may be less circumscribed as to time, and fortunate are they who, having leisure, can support the rarefied air of Madrid long enough to do justice to the greatest picture-gallery in the world. It is not only the greatest but the best-arranged, the quietest and the most comfortable. You leave your carriage at the door and stroll in for an hour or so. All is quiet, and silent, and orderly as in a church; the rooms are unadorned and perfectly lighted; the pictures are never hidden by crowds of copyists; the place is never crowded or noisy; and after contemplating your favourite pictures or picture for a time, you leave the gallery, not tired and blinded by too many impressions, but refreshed and invigorated with a calm intellectual enjoyment that is as good and simple as it is deep and lasting.

CHAPTER V.

A LEAR OF CITIES.—GOTHIC, ROMAN, AND MOORISH REMAINS.—COMMENTARIES ON STREET'S GOTHIC ARCHITECTURE, AND ON TOLEDAN LANDLORDS.—TILES, AND A DISCOURSE THEREON.

THE railway journey from Madrid to Toledo is easy enough, occupying about eight hours. Time is given for refreshment on the way, and you are almost certain to be alone if you travel first-class, which, if you are a wise traveller, you will be sure to do. Every one knows how much easier it is to take long journeys in an uncrowded vehicle, and by following this precaution always we saved up strength for future ordeal.

Toledo looks imposing from the railway station, but it is the dirtiest, dreariest, most uncomfortable town in the world. We were driven from the station at a furious rate in the diligence drawn by four mules, and the driver lashed them so furiously and vociferated so franticly that we thought he must be mad or drunk. Over the bridge we went at a galloping rate, and so on, up-hill, down-hill, till we reached the town. Here, at least, I thought, we should stop in our mad career, for the streets of Toledo, like all Moorish streets, are mere bridle-tracks, paved with flint-stone; and as the town, like Rome, is built on seven hills, you are always ascending or descending. But our driver never slackened whip or reins for one moment; and, wonderful to say, the cumbersome vehicle emerged safely from break-neck alleys which looked hardly wide enough for a wheelbarrow. With such dash, indeed, did we drive into the court-yard of the Hôtel de Leno that we had taken the flattering unction to our souls that we were very welcome guests. But on alighting no one took any notice of us; and, though the master of the house, with a staff of waiters and maids, were standing about, it never seemed to occur to them that we needed their services. There we stood in the midst of our luggage—two portmanteaus and ten packages of smaller dimensions—for about a quarter of an hour, when the landlord came up and with a civil manner conducted us to our rooms. This apparent uncourteousness meant nothing more than Spanish indifference, as we afterwards found out, for never were we better treated than in this same Fonda de Leno. Finding that we objected to dine in the smoky *salle-à-manger*, the master himself served us in our rooms, and served us, I believe, to the best of his ability. He was a heavy-looking man, and his manners at first were a little disconcerting, but we liked him on better acquaintance, and he chatted a good deal about English travellers. I think our patience and smattering of "Castellano" won his good graces. The house was scrupulously clean, and the food, though ultra-Spanish, quite good enough for any one excepting an epicure.

Toledo boasts of an excellent guide, without whom the traveller would fare ill there, despite clean beds and wholesome food. What a debt of gratitude do we not owe to you, good Señor Cabezas, for having guided us so well through this more than Cretan myth—not I am sure from gain's sake only, but from an honest antiquarian love of it! "I am a son of Toledo, *hijo de Toledo*," he said to us; "and there is not a stone of the place unknown to me:" and this speech was made without any self-arrogance or vanity. It was the simple truth. There is this good trait about the Spaniard of the lower ranks, that he never affects, and is consequently never a snob. He treats you—a little too familiarly, I daresay, to please aristocratic palates—but always with a quiet dignity and self-possession, reminding you of the Arabs, and most likely inherited from them. How much, indeed, has not the Spaniard inherited from the Arab?

Señor Cabezas is a slightly-built, prematurely old man, with eyes of extraordinary vivacity, very small hands and feet (a veritable *cosa de España*), and a chronic cough that makes one think the climate of Toledo does not suit her son. He carries a stick, with which he points out any precious relic that comes in the way, and is so peremptory and so like a schoolmaster in making you understand the history of it, that you dread lest the stick should descend upon your knuckles or shoulders if guilty of inattention. But only really idle people would deserve the stick, for Cabezas thoroughly understands what he is talking about, and, like all wise men, reserves his talk for occasions worthy of it. You are never wearied by him, but follow his eyes and the point of the stick with unflagging interest.

Cabezas is always busy, and we had to accept thankfully as much of his time as he could spare.

"I have engaged myself this afternoon," he said, "to an old French gentleman, a silk-merchant bound to Murcia, but, if you like, you can accompany us in our rounds." This we did, and the silk-merchant proved not only an inoffensive, but a very amusing person.

The poor man seemed so tormented with the idea of seeing all the sights of Toledo that one would have fancied he was thereby doing penance for his sins. When he found himself in the Cathedral, his melancholy became overwhelming. The beautiful painted windows, the richly-carved stalls of the choir, the exquisite Retablo, the chapels, each so full of monuments and treasures, the pictures, relics, and jewels of the Sacristy, and the *coup d'œils* of the whole interior, could only elicit from him a dreary expression of regret that there was so much to see.

As we were led from chapel to chapel, he raised his hands and repeated, " Il y a trop à voir, il y a trop à voir"—which was perfectly true. There is too much to see, but then why not accept the fact cheerfully? To see every part of the Cathedral of Toledo would indeed require weeks, and to describe it, even in general terms, would fill a volume. I advise all travellers who have no time for a series of visits, or a scrupulous reading of many books, to go into the Cathedral alone and read nothing about it whatever. By following this plan you obtain one distinct and ineffaceable impression, whilst a hurried visit, with a garrulous *cicerone* at your heels, and a guide-book in your hands, results in very little but mortification. Grateful as we felt to good Señor Cabezas for his painstaking services, we were never so happy in the grand old place, as when we stole in by ourselves at early morning and twilight. Nothing then marred the prevailing impression of splendour and beauty; and we wandered up and down the quiet aisles, and looked at the tiers of gorgeously-coloured windows, lost in a rapture of wonder and delight.

I do not remember to have seen any finer sight in Europe than the interior of Toledo Cathedral; the whole is so magnificent, the detail so harmonious, the colouring so beautiful; such an impression never fades from the mind's eye, but remains "a thing of joy," and a storehouse of beauty, for ever.

It is a great pity that the exquisite chapels are so disfigured with images and altars dressed up in every form and fashion of tinsel. You are taken too to see the jewels and wardrobe of the Virgin—the strangest sight. It is difficult to reconcile the character of the lowly Mother of Christ with these gorgeous robes of velvet and brocade, stiff with gold and pearls, with these necklets, rings, and bracelets; with these tiaras of diamonds and emeralds. But everywhere you see the same thing, only on a smaller scale; the Virgin is petted and pampered with costly gifts as if she were something below an ordinary woman, since even ordinary women aspire to higher things than a fine toilette.

There was a homely German lady in the Sacristy with us, who had surveyed the aisles very calmly, but went into raptures over these jewelled mantles and petticoats.

"*Himmel!*" she said, touching the rich stuffs gingerly with her fingers, "what a pity such beautiful things are not worn ; the silks must have cost six thalers a-yard at least."

Putting aside the idea of profanity, no one can help enjoying the blaze of so many gems. It is like walking in Aladdin's enchanted garden. Diamonds, emeralds, pearls, sapphires, rubies, are here collected in such masses, that one's eyes get too dazzled and blinded at last to see any more. Nor does the treasure-house of the Cathedral stop here. There is a fabulous amount of gold and silver in the form of candelabras, urns, reliquaries and *incensarios*, or vessels for holding incense ; there is an altar composed of pure amber ; there are banners heavy with gold and precious stones, relics of saints more precious to the good Catholic than any jewels, and last, not least, illuminated Bibles and missals blazing with gold.

Well might the silk-merchant raise his hands and sigh, "There is too much to see !" I think it would take a month to see all these wonderful things fairly, and more than that to master their history. Then there are the sacred legends which would, doubtless, outnumber the Virgin's pearls and diamonds, and are of infinite more comfort to the humblest of her worshippers. And how beautiful and tender are some of them! that, for instance, of the shrine of San Ildefonso. San Ildefonso was the primate of Toledo, and one day the Virgin came down from heaven to attend matins at the Cathedral. It all happened on a sudden, as miracles do. A moment before, the place had been empty, now it was filled—by whom? Could it be any other than the Mother of God, with those sweet eyes, that golden hair, that shining aureole around her head? Think of the awe, and bewilderment, and pious joy of the people worshipping there, especially the poor, who thrill with pride at sight of an earthly Queen. How they must have wept and wondered then! how they must have wept and smiled at repeating the story afterwards!

It is thirteen hundred years since this took place; the marble slab where the Virgin's feet alighted has been hollowed with the kisses of thousands of worshippers, and the story moves to tears of joy still. No one can help feeling the enduring power of these old church legends before such evidence, and no one can help being, for the time, carried away by their simple pathos or burning faith. You should never travel in Spain without a book about the saints and martyrs. Every step you take leads across some way watered with holy blood and tears. Every town is peopled with the sorrowful ghosts of men and women whom the Church has tried and crowned; and only those who are obstinately blind can deny the influence exercised by their names still. Often and often have I found myself, as in the convent of *Las Huelgas*, realising the religious spirit of the middle ages in its vigour and purity. But, alas! only for a little while, and I think the most devout Romanist would hardly find Spain the country of his expectation.

Excepting the Cathedral, nearly all the glories of Toledo are Moorish. The Moors, those true artists and most conscientious workers, have here left an Alcazar, gateways, bridges, mosques, palaces, and towers, to perpetuate their golden age; and though the grand old metropolitan church remains the crowning jewel of the desolate old city (a Lear of cities, deaf, blind, decaying), all these anticipate the marvels of Cordova and Granada. But the Cathedral takes you back to quite another epoch of art and religion. Pass along the tortuous street called the Calle de la Chapinerier, and enter the north transept, and you might fancy yourself in one of the early Gothic churches of France.

The view into the double aisles round the choir across the magnificent Capilla Mayor, and down the side aisles of the nave, is superb, whilst the atmosphere of the whole place, so dusky, and twilight always, gives wonderful solemnity to the whole. The windows are large and numerous, but all are filled with beautiful stained glass, so that not a ray falls that is not quite marvellous in beauty of colours. The choir and aisles are arranged in three gradations of height, and the effect of the three tiers of coloured windows is full of charm. It is in the intermediate aisle that the practised eye recognises at a glance the influence of the Moor, for the arcade of the triforium has the unmistakeable horse-shoe arch; and very beautiful is the effect, and testifying to the good sense of the architect who so wisely imitated what was good in foreign art.

Spend hours in wandering from aisle to aisle from chapel to chapel, till you have mastered the grand outline of the architect in all its simplicity and perfection, and then how much yet remains to study! There is the beautiful arrangement of columns, about which Mr. Street writes so enthusiastically, the noble rose-window of the transept, the doorway of St. Catharine with its elaborate mouldings, the screens round the Coro, the chapel of San Ildefonso with its richly-sculptured tombs, all remarkable as specimens of fourteenth century work; then there are the cloister and chapel of San Blas; the chapel of Santiago, great and interesting works of the fifteenth century; the massive brass and iron screens, the grand and gorgeous Retablos, and lastly, the beautiful stained glass medallions of all periods. What treasures of tradition, of thought, of time, are here! Who leaves Toledo without a regret that none can be properly studied in a passing visit?

The cathedrals of Burgos and Toledo were all that we were able to see of Gothic architecture in Spain, but these more than fulfilled any expectations held out to us. Toledo, I presume, equals any church in Europe in the grandeur of its plan and the beauty of every part; and certainly surpasses any I have seen for solemnity. I would fain set out on another pilgrimage at some future time, to see the Cathedrals of Leon, Segovia, Salamanca, and the beautiful old churches of Cataluña. Indeed, so rich is Spain in ecclesiastical architecture, often exotic, but belonging to her by right of possession nevertheless, and so more than rich in church furniture, that such a journey would be unequalled in interest and instruction. Think for a moment of the treasures scattered by the way. There are the magnificent Retablos of Salamanca and Gerona, richly sculptured and covered with gold, with silver and with painting; there are the elaborately carved choir stalls of Toledo and Valencia, the sumptuous monuments of Avila, Miraflores, and Burgos, the exquisite screens or Rejas in metal, so plentiful in all the churches, curious old organs, carved doors and ceilings, regal magnificence and abundant labour manifested everywhere.

What is very curious in the history of Moorish and Christian art in Spain, is their distinction from each other. The two arts ran in parallel lines; and whilst the Moors were building the Mosque at Cordova, the Alcazar and Giralda at Seville, and the Alhambra, the Christians were raising the beautiful Gothic churches so thickly scattered all over the country. To this rule there are, of course, exceptions; such for instance as the triforium of the choir at Toledo, which is decidedly Moorish in design, the Moorish carpentry plentifully found in late Gothic buildings, the Moorish battlement constantly seen on the walls of Spanish towns; and there are other examples, though none on the whole of importance. The Moors and Christians were alternately conquerors and vanquished, and always enemies; so that it was not to be expected that they should have copied each other's art, however ready they might be to adopt modifications of it. The Moorish builders and architects often worked for and with their Christian masters; and this accounts for the Moorish elements predominant in the streets and buildings of such a city as Toledo. But the arts of the two people remained as separate as their languages.

Toledo is a most bewildering place, and without good Señor Cabezas, the traveller would find himself lost in every sense. The streets are thoroughly Moorish, tortuous, narrow, steep, and ill-paved; and you might fancy yourself in Algiers in any one of these dark alleys, so admirably built for coolness, seclusion, and security. You might fancy yourself in Algiers, or indeed, in any Eastern city, on other accounts, especially the singing,—that monotonous, dreary, interminable singing you hear everywhere among the Arabs. The Spaniard, among other things, has borrowed of the Oriental those dreary "howlings of Tarshish,"* which in Toledo, in Cordova, and in Granada, recall the East, if the East has come within

* The name of Tarshish is supposed to have been applied to the kingdom of Andalusia.

your range of travel, and if not, set you wondering whence so lively a people acquired so melancholy a kind of recreation. Anything more depressing than these same "howlings of Tarshish" cannot be conceived. If you are in a thoroughly Spanish inn you hear them incessantly from morning to night. The servants begin hours before you rise, the children of the house take up the strain, master and mistress sing over their cookery and ledger-writing, stable-boy and gardener sing over their work without. Strive as you may, you cannot get away from the sound. It is better to sing yourself, and then you like it.

Again, setting aside the old Moorish houses still remaining, you find that the modern Toledans have built on the same plan, shutting themselves up within four walls like true Orientals, and delighting their eyes with foliage and fountain in sunny courts. But the beautiful precept of cleanliness is not imposed on the Toledans as it was on the Moors, and everywhere one regrets it. The streets are filthy, and so rugged that they make you lame in an hour; and yet there is so much to see that, lame or no, you must keep walking on.

What irritates you beyond endurance is the culpable neglect of everything valuable to both historian and antiquary. Ruin runs riot as she pleases, and not a hand is put forth to stay her progress. Inlaid ceilings of cedar-wood, delicate diapers of plaster-work, pavements of beautiful tiles,—all are allowed to go to ruin; and they go so fast, that my advice to all interested in the wonderful Moorish antiquities of Toledo is, that they should see them at once. A few years hence there will be none to see.

Cabezas, who has a genuine love of what is really good in art and curious in antiquities, bewailed with us this cruel contempt of both on the part of his countrymen. There was something quite touching in the way he lingered over every relic, as if it were a living thing fading before his eyes. It is the same with every kind of artistic or archæological treasure, Roman, Gothic, and Moorish, all share the same fate. I don't think Spaniards, as a rule, care much for what the Moors left behind them; rather it is cavilled at and despised.

A few years ago a most precious treasure-trove was discovered near Toledo and sold—oh! indifferent Spain!—to the Emperor of the French. It consisted of five or six crowns, with crosses suspended to them, and three smaller ones without crosses,—all of pure gold, beautifully worked and adorned with jewels. These crowns, now exhibited in the Hôtel de Cluny, are relics of the Gothic kings of Spain, and are evidently votive crowns, of the age of Recesvinthus, and the episcopate of San Ildefonso; and, though belonging to a very early period of art, about 650–672, exhibit extraordinary knowledge of the goldsmith's art. Doubtless, from time to time, other *reliquiæ*, quite as interesting, will come to light; but what will become of them, Heaven only knows.

I don't know which phase of Spanish history is most generally interesting—the Mahomedan, the Catholic, or the Aristocratic: the former being typified in the Alhambra, the second in the paintings of Murillo and Zurbaran, and the third in the splendid courts of the Philips. I confess that for me the Mahomedan phase, so graceful, so artistic, so beneficent as it was, surpasses in interest every other. Look a little into the history of Spain, and what do facts tell you? To whom is she indebted for her most sumptuous monuments, her most fertile districts, her most elegant arts, her most picturesque costumes, her most precious products?—To the Moors. Who brought down the cool waters from rocky prisons, turning whole wastes into sunny vineyards and gardens?—The Moors. Who built bridges, fortifications, and watch-towers? — The Moors. Who made the Spanish language what it is now, the most sonorous and picturesque of any in Europe?—The Moors. Who planted the orange-tree and the palm, the fig and the olive?—The Moors.

One cannot help crying out against the ingratitude of the Spaniards, who not only disclaim the good things thus inherited, but do their best to defile them. Nowhere is this defilement more obvious than at Toledo. It is as if everything Moorish were infected with the plague.

A wonderful lesson in history is this dreary old Spanish town, and offering food enough and to spare for the hungry antiquary. Toledo may be called a palimpsest; in its outermost surface is the

Spanish writing, clear, and new, and plain; scratch it, and you see the Moorish, all glowing in colour and gold; scratch deeper, and you have the stately Roman; deeper. still, the rude Gothic; deeper still, the barbaric Carthaginian. Take up a handful of dust, and who can say what it is— ashes of Roman prætors, Gothic kings, or Moorish patrons of art and science? Or cast your eyes over the vast panorama of bridge and gateway, watch-tower and church, fort and pleasure-ground—which of these is not as much Roman as Moorish, more Moorish than Christian, and has not first belonged to an earlier civilization than either?

Nothing more forcibly recalls the East than the embroidered mule-trappings one meets at every step. Here in Toledo, as in all Moorish cities, the mules are as gorgeously dressed up as if each belonged to a prince; and, with that inexhaustible invention and love of ornament one finds among Orientals, no two trappings are made alike. These bits of colour in some measure redeem the monotony of the streets, which are tiring both to feet and eyes. All the beauties are hidden in ugly backgrounds, like toads' eyes, and without a good guide you would never find them out. With such helps as Ford, Street, and good Señor Cabezas, the intelligent traveller need not remain ignorant of any; and though the relics of Moorish art may not have the attractions for every one that they had for us, none can but admire the exquisite little mosque turned into a place for Christian worship, the superb ceilings of cedar-wood, blue and white, the arches, courts, doors, tiles, and other *disjecta membra* of the age of the royal race of Granada long passed away.

We were particularly interested in the beautiful encaustic tiles, of which one sees so many specimens here. Cabezas very obligingly took us to a private house rich in this sort of ornament, and we spent the whole afternoon in copying the prettiest specimens. The master and mistress were handsome young people who seemed to have nothing to do but laugh and talk in their balcony, overlooking the *patio* where we sat. It was a very pretty place, so Eastern in colour and character. The court was open to the sky, the floor was of coloured tiles, the walls pure white above and gay with tiles below, whilst overhead burned and glowed a bright blue Southern sky.

Our host and hostess watched us at our work with child-like curiosity, and quizzing us not a little. "What curious people are they, these English! What in the world do they want to copy our tiles for?" said the lady, and the husband answered, "To sell 'em, I suppose." "Come now, Señor Cabezas," said the lady, "and tell us who these ladies are, and what they come here to paint for? I should think they might find something better to do than paint a few old Moorish tiles." Cabezas explained apologetically that we were tourists much interested in anything Moorish, that one of us had a house in Algiers, that we had come to Spain on purpose to see the beautiful ruins of Toledo and Granada, and so forth.

"But how queerly they dress! Do all English ladies wear those funny things on their heads instead of mantillas?—And then they don't wear chignons: what frights they look, to be sure!"

To be sure there is no accounting for tastes: we had thought the immense lumps of wool and false hair worn by Spanish women of all classes anything but pretty.

The lady had a hundred more questions to ask, the great object of inquiry seeming to be the relationship between my companion and myself.

"It's impossible they can be sisters," she observed, "for one is twice as big as the other."

"Oh! what has that to do with it?" rejoined her husband; "one often sees sisters as unlike each other as can be."

"Well, I should say," the lady went on, "that the tall one with the golden hair is no relation to the little one whatever—unless it be her brother's wife." And finally they settled it so.

Meantime we got on admirably with our work, and made copies of several very beautiful tiles. Before coming away, the lady of the house descended from the balcony to look at them and us.

"They are very pretty," she said, turning over the drawings one by one; "but what are they good for?"

"We want to compare them with those in the

Alhambra and in the old Moorish buildings in Algeria," we said, " to see which are the prettiest."

She seemed by no means convinced.

" But what does it matter which is the prettiest ?"

To this, of course, we found no satisfactory answer. What, indeed, does anything about anything matter to some people ? and to the little Spanish lady, like Peter Bell, a Moorish tile and a primrose was a Moorish tile and a primrose—nothing more.

My friend did a little sketching out-of-doors and was sure to have a little crowd round her. In most cases it would be grave, portly, well-dressed peasants, who came to look on, and their behaviour was always respectful and intelligent. I liked the look of these Castilian farmers and shepherds, who wear their sheepskin, or coarse brown woollen rug bordered with colours over their shoulders with quite a noble air. They would come up to us, say simply " Buenos dias," and then stand by, without either impertinence or apology. This pleasant freedom of manner, alike removed from obsequiousness or vulgarity, strikes a foreigner as much as the fine, thoughtful Velasquez face he often sees among the Castilian peasantry.

Once it was a dozen schoolboys who gathered round the English Señora to see what she was drawing. They were just coming home from school, and, by way of keeping them out of my companion's light, I drew them aside and asked to look at their books. This seemed to create no little amusement; but when I opened a grammar and began a random examination, there was a chorus of laughter. It was a very learned and dry grammar that these young Toledans, all apparently of the lower classes, had to learn; but they seemed to know it very well. And there were also dry books of a theological tendency, besides a catechism and a history. No wonder Toledo remains orthodox in religion and grammar, when the sons of artisans and peasants are instructed so exclusively in both. It is said that here the noble Castilian tongue is spoken in all its purity; a matter in which the passing traveller is hardly able to judge, but the multitude of priests thronging the streets bespeaks the thoroughgoing Catholicism of the place. Despite the railway and the increased number of travellers it brings, an English lady seems to be as much an object of curiosity here as ever; and though the curiosity is not ill-natured, it rather spoils the enjoyment of one's walks. Yet one is obliged to walk from morning to night; there is so much to see, and as *fiacres* are not to be heard of, there is no other way of getting about. The streets are not picturesque in themselves, but the view of the vast, scattered, decayed, and decaying old city, with its grand gates, walls, and bridges, from the Alcazar to the river side, is extraordinarily fine. The Tagus is a narrow, deep green stream, which runs amid dark rocks of rugged and fantastic shape: or waters soft green *vegas*, the sweeter, because so rare. Hardly the Tiber is more historic, and one leaves its banks lingeringly.

We had not seen half enough of Toledo when we came away, and should have stayed longer but for the cold. It was warm and brilliant all day long; but when evening came, and, tired and footsore, we reached our Fonda, the cold seemed insupportable. There were no fireplaces anywhere, and no other means of heating the room but a charcoal-pan, which is a wretched contrivance, never of use except when so heated as to be dangerous. We took refuge, as usual, in our soft, clean beds, and, by dint of rugs and wraps, contrived to get warm at last.

CHAPTER VI.

A MIDNIGHT HALT.—ITS CHARMS AND COUNTER-CHARMS.—DON QUIXOTE'S COUNTRY.—THE SLEEP AT CORDOVA.—THE WAKE IN THE EAST.—SHOPPING.

T was with real regret we left Toledo, as one leaves some rare old book, only glanced at, but enticing months' study. Notwithstanding the depressing gloom and stagnation of the old city, we loved it for its beautiful and precious monuments, and for the historic solemnity hanging round each. We liked the people too—Cabezas our invaluable guide; our hotel-keeper; Pepa, our bright little chambermaid; and the homely but respectful waiters, who were so slow to understand what we wanted, and so slow to bring it when understood. When you leave a Spanish Fonda there is none of that obsequious crowding round you that you find in France

and England. Chambermaids and waiters never hover about you, hinting by their looks that they expect vails, but say simply "Adios, adios," and go their ways.

But I especially dwell on the civility we met with at the Fonda de Leno, because we afterwards heard it so terribly abused. We were dining at the *table d'hôte* at Granada, and a party of American travellers began talking of fondas in general, and of the fondas at Toledo in particular.

"I shan't easily forget the boorishness of the landlord," said one; "I really thought he would have turned us clean out-of-doors. Why, we civilly asked what there was for breakfast, and he said 'Eel and chops,' and turned on his heel without asking which we chose to have! And what cooking! everything tasted of tomatoes and garlic!"

"And what wretched rooms!" put in a young lady; "as bare of furniture as prisons."

There were two young Frenchmen present who had also been at Toledo, and they now joined in the cry. They were starved, unhandsomely treated, badly housed, overcharged.

"But there *is* a comfortable hotel at Toledo," I

said; "we found very good food, moderate charges, and such civil people, at the Hôtel de Leno."

There was a general exclamation of surprise.

"That is the very place we are complaining of!" they all said; and we compared notes with as much perplexity as amusement.

I don't at all understand the usual tone taken by tourists in describing Spanish inns. We never found anything to complain of, and yet how few people admit the possibility of ladies travelling comfortably in Spain! Carry with you a tolerable supply of patience and gold pieces, you will do very well. Carry with you, also, always ready for use, a little courteous *Castellano*, which will often stand in good stead of many more costly things, such as time, money, and temper. Moreover, reverse the Micawber principle, and never expect anything to turn up, for that will save many a discomfort to yourself and others. The Spaniards are terribly slow and procrastinating, but the fact must be accepted as it is, and made the best of; as well expect an American to be lethargic as a Spaniard to be quick.

From Toledo to Cordova is a very long railway journey. You have to wait from seven o'clock in the evening till midnight to catch the down train from Madrid, which waiting might, of course, be easily avoided. Fancy waiting five or six hours at Didcot for the Leamington train! But *mañana, mañana,* all the good changes will take place in time!

We found the waiting at Castilejo not so bad as might be. Tourists had said to us with a shrug of the shoulders, "It is a terrible ordeal to go through, that waiting at Castilejo. There will, very likely, be neither fire nor light, and you will have to choose between a dark hole of a waiting-room, full of men smoking, or get into an empty railway-carriage and wait there."

We certainly were agreeably surprised to find a blazing fire; a room that, if not exceptionally clean, was at least airy and wholesome; and instead of the crowd of smokers we had been led to expect, a young Madrid lady with her maid and dog, two or three respectable servant girls, and one elderly railway guard, who might have been Don Quixote, he was so grim and so gallant. The girls dropped off to sleep one by one; the guard puffed away his inoffensive little cigarette deep in thought, and we got out our books and amused ourselves very well. There was a livelier scene at the buffet just behind the waiting-room, for, when I went to beg an extra light and to ask for chocolate, I found a number of soldiers and peasants regaling on hot little bits of meat that came, as if by magic, from behind the counter.

The young woman in attendance was, as usual, civil but indifferent.

"Have you chocolate?" I asked.

"I don't think we have, Señora," she replied; "I'll see by-and-by."

"Have you chocolate?" I asked, when the by-and-by had come.

"I don't think we have, Señora," was the answer a second time; "I'll see by-and-by."

I waited a little while, and then repeated the question, always in the politest way possible. This time I added that the Señora with me was very tired, and sadly in need of refreshment, and that if there was chocolate to be had I should be very much obliged.

"The mistress of the Fonda is gone to bed, and I don't know where she keeps the chocolate," was the reply this time; 'but I have sent to hear, and if there is any you shall be served.'

About two hours from the time of my first inquiry came two delicious little cups of chocolate, which, I am sure, we should never have got except by means of patience and pretty speeches. The traveller who has not a goodly supply of both these things would, I fear, fare very ill. After a time the sleepers woke up, and began to talk in very lively fashion. A smart young lady, who seemed to belong to the station, soon came in, wished everybody " buenas noches," and sat down, evidently with the intention of being amused. The young lady and her maid did not hold aloof from the conversation, the grave-looking guard joined in occasionally, and the two English ladies were not excluded.

The young women, who wore black silk mantillas, and chignons as large as cocoa-nuts, were immensely inquisitive about English ladies in general, and ourselves in particular. When we had satisfied their curiosity, we talked of *Cosas de España*, mantillas, fans, bull-fights, &c.

"Now, tell me," I said to the young lady belonging to the station, "do you really like bull-fights or no? I have never heard the opinion of a Spanish lady on the subject."

"That is, because foreigners make such a fuss about bull-fights," she replied, archly; "people are afraid to speak their minds about it. For my part, I own that the sight is a horrid one, but it amuses me."

"It don't amuse me," put in one girl; "I get sick and frightened, and want to come away."

"Well," added another, "it's all very well for people to say they don't like it; they go all the same. These English Señoras went, I'll be bound; and yet they'll go back to England and talk about us."

My companion shook her head. I pleaded guilty.

"But," I said in extenuation, "I only went to convince myself, with my own eyes, that the sport is so popular as travellers report. I couldn't have believed it otherwise."

Meantime train after train came and went, the train to Badajoz, the train to Alicante, the train to Saragosa, and, at last, the one which was to bear us to Cordova. There it came, creeping through the darkness with its big red eyes, like some monster of Eastern fable, but much more kindly, for it gave us what we needed—quiet, and sleep, and solitude. As usual, we found the ladies' coupé empty, and, as usual, we curled ourselves up in our rugs, wished each other " good night," and went to sleep.

There is a cant phrase about railways having done away with the poetry of travelling. Was ever such an absurdity uttered and believed in? I think if ever the poetry of travel was realised, it is now, especially at night and in Spain. You are whirled from region to region apparently by elemental fire alone. You pass through new, sweet, starry atmospheres, like a bird; you go to sleep, and never know under what strange or happy auspices you will awake. This beautiful moonlight landscape of tiny homesteads lying on the banks of a silvery river, of green meadows skirting snow-tipped mountains, and long lines of fir-trees pricking against a blue-black sky,—is it real or a picture only? These dreary table-lands that seem to stretch into infinity, these sloping olive-grounds, these sharp sierras, these alternating scenes of loveliness, and grandeur, and desolation, seem more like the phantasmagoria of dreams than anything else.

And then the aspects of human life, though fleeting, are yet so full of charm. You see faces that tell their own story, and in a moment they have vanished. You are let into little domestic scenes touching, or comic, or painful, or passionate, as the case may be. You cannot stop five minutes at a village station, or linger five minutes in a village waiting-room, without being moved to smiles or tears.

For my part I have never taken a railway journey, however short, that has not had some incident worth remembering; but in Spain, which is a collection of kingdoms, each rich in different sorts of interest, one is troubled, like the silk-merchant at Toledo, with the *embarras de richesses*. You see a hundred landscapes in a day you would fain remember. You see a hundred faces and hear a hundred things, that seem too characteristic to forget. But, like the changing colours of the sunset, these impressions melt one into the other, and, unless seized at the moment, are utterly lost.

When day broke we found that we were traversing a mountainous region of olive-orchards and bare brown fields made ready for sowing, some no larger than a cottager's garden, others covering acres. A tawny land is this Spain, as Shakespeare says, a gipsy among gipsies, and a Moor by complexion.

We were now in Don Quixote's country,—such a dreary country, that every one should take Cervantes' book to read on the way. Then La Mancha, though a mere waste of steppes, with here and there wretched mud-hovels, becomes enchanted ground, and every village named on the map, as sacred as Mecca. "Never let Don Quixote be out of our reader's saddle-bags," says *the* guide to Spain; "it is the best HAND-BOOK to La Mancha, moral and geographical; there is nothing in it imaginary except the hero's monomania."

What is more real than fiction after all ?

The battle-fields of Spain are not more interesting than the spots immortalized by Cervantes' marvellous novel, and one longs to make a pilgrimage to each. As we glide through the charmed region, how familiar do the names and aspects of places seem to us? We are near the village of El Toboso, where lived Dulcinea, whose real name was said to be Aldonza Corchuelo; we pass group after group of windmills, any of which are grim enough to appear like giants to a madman now; here the Don was knighted, there he did penance; amid those craggy heights of the Sierra Morena, he found Cardenio; there glides the stream in which beautiful Dorothea bathed her feet. New names, new faces, new associations, seem alone untrue, unreal, and out of place; and we live all day in Don Quixote's country among Don Quixote's friends; Dulcinea, the hospitable goatherd, the wicked little Duchess, the homely Maritornes, the curate and the niece, all are here; and we look across the brown lines of the table-land, and see, or seem to see, the Don himself, spare and spectre-like, followed by burly Sancho Panza, riding out in search of adventure.

There are some who say that *Don Quixote* should be eaten and drunk on Spanish ground, or its delicate flavour is wholly lost. For my part, I think if ever a book could bear translation and transportation, it is Cervantes' novel of novels.

There is nothing like it in any literature,—so new, so true, and so wonderful. What would life be without it? Take away the charms of style and the beauties of a language rare in beauties, and yet all remains that we most care for. Don Quixote, Sancho Panza, as creations, are too simple and too true to stand or fall by the ordinary test. Why, *Don Quixote* translated into a language as rude as that of Fighi islanders, would be every inch *Don Quixote* still, and of what other novel can so much be said? Few travellers will omit Cervantes' Biography from their saddle-bags. He was the noblest of noble Spaniards, and his life shines like a diamond without one flaw. What a sad life, too! Even *Don Quixote*, the blossom of his riper intellect, brought no good fortune with it.

We leave La Mancha, and now the scene wholly changes. The air becomes soft and balmy; we see a garden of roses here, a cluster of palms there; white villages at the feet of green hills; sunny streams and golden sunshine everywhere. We are in Andalusia!

We had been recommended by our hotel-keeper in Madrid to the Hôtel Suisse, and, notwithstanding his recommendation, entered its walls with fear and trembling. The English gentleman's words rang yet in our ears, "Don't sleep at Cordova!" and we could hardly believe our eyes when we drove into a pretty Moorish court, with flowers and orange-trees and a fountain in the midst, and light galleries running round, all white and shining as if of marble. But, after all, this might be only the whitewashing of the sepulchre. We forbore any exclamation of surprise, and asked to see our rooms. A respectable-looking chambermaid led the way to three very well-furnished, clean, and airy rooms, in which we installed ourselves, feeling no longer any apprehension of discomfort.

Indeed, we found everything good at Cordova, —attendance, beds, and food; we had nice coffee or chocolate in our own rooms at seven o'clock, a breakfast of cold game, omelettes, cutlets, and fruit at mid-day, and an excellent *table d'hôte* dinner in the evening. Of course, we did not get, or expect to get, anything like English dishes; but we found the Spanish ones eatable and nutritious, and *quid multa?* I only allude to this subject, because it is a fashion to rail against Spanish inns, and, I think, unjustly. The charges are not higher than in Paris or Vienna, and the accommodation, in most cases, very good. You are not mulcted largely in the matter of vails, and though the servants are slow, they are obliging, and we found them, at least, honest.

The dilatoriness is very amusing. For instance, on the eve of quitting Cordova, we rang for our bill, ordering, at the same time, a basket of provisions to take with us. The summons was answered pretty promptly, and we were assured that our orders should be obeyed forthwith. After waiting a good hour, we rang again, for we were to rise next morning at five o'clock, and wished to go to bed. This time another waiter appeared, who seemed, however, to have a clear notion of what we wanted; and vanished, promising to see to things himself. Another hour passed, no bill, no basket, no trace of either; and as it was now ten o'clock, a very late hour for travellers, we determined to countermand the order, and stand our chance of procuring provisions by the way. But the third ring was answered to more purpose.

First came the bill, borne by the head-waiter;

secondly, came a pair of roast partridges, steaming hot; thirdly, a loaf of bread: then there was a solemn pause of about a quarter of an hour, at the end of which time we got our change, our basket with the remaining provisions, and quiet for the night! Fancy, a simple order like this requiring nearly three hours for its execution anywhere but in Spain!

The best plan is to carry about with you an amusing novel, and take it up whenever you have to wait for anything or anybody. Scolding does no good,—rather, I think, aggravates the evil. At least, we never found that we were worse off than other people who did scold.

But I must go back to the time of our arrival. Cordova is a brighter and more bustling place than Toledo, and more Oriental. The houses, the dress, the handicrafts, the tools, and the songs, are thoroughly Arab; the climate is soft, the sky clear and southern, and flowers are out as if it were June!

Here, too, one sees plenty of costume. The sheepskin jacket, the national *sombrero*, the brilliant sash, the beautifully-embroidered gaiters of Cordova leather. The women, for the most part, wear cheap cotton dresses that have evidently come from Manchester, but the mantilla and fan are always used at mass.

We were too late to see inside the Mosque that afternoon, and having looked longingly at its beautiful old walls, now mellowed to a deep orange by the setting sun, we strolled to the bridge. Never, I think, have I seen a picture more sweet and peaceful. The Guadalquivir (how Arabic does the word sound as pronounced here!) reflected an opal sky, that changed from violet to pink, and from pink to pale daffodil. The olive-clad slopes lay in tender shadow, and beyond river, and bridge, and roof, rose the dark ridge of the Sierra Morena. The air was so warm that we sat down by the river-side till the colours died out of the sky and landscape, and the grave and beautiful twilight enveloped all. Then we went home to our comfortable inn, and brought out our books, and read so much of the glories of Cordova, that we dreamed all night that we were living in the times of Haroun Al Raschid. Why describe what has been described so often and so well? In these days, when every one travels, and every one who does not travel, reads the experience of others, it would seem, then, useless to supplement Ford, and Borrow, and Gautier, and all the clever writers who have gone over the same ground. But it is impossible to write of Spain, and leave out Cordova, the Carthaginian capital, the rival of Cadiz in wealth and traffic, the birthplace of the Senecas, of Lucan, and of Averroes; alike the Athens and the Bagdad of the West; and the seat of a Caliphate, whose story reads like a page of the *Arabian Nights*. We can understand how the Moors came to love Andalusia, and make it their home, planting the palm, the orange, and the vine, building mosque, and palace, and tower, turning into a paradise the lovely land they had sought in exile. A thousand years ago, the Ommiad Caliphs, descendants of a lonely refugee, ruled in a splendid city containing a million of inhabitants, three hundred mosques, nine hundred baths, six hundred inns, and all the elegancies and refinements of the most graceful civilization the world has yet seen. The Arabian historian, Al-Makkari, describes, in glowing words, "the running streams, limpid waters, luxuriant gardens, stately buildings, magnificent palaces, throngs of soldiers, pages, eunuchs, and slaves of all nations and religions, sumptuously attired in robes of silk and brocade; crowds of judges and Katib, theologians and poets, walking with becoming gravity, through the magnificent halls, spacious ante-rooms, and ample courts of the palace;" and having gone on to describe the ruin that overtook all, adds, with true Mahomedan resignation, "There is no God but Allah, the great, the Almighty!" And what is Cordova now, once the learned, the luxurious, the aristocratic? "It withered under the Spaniard," says Mr. Ford, with pardonable sarcasm, "and, rich and learned under Roman and Moor, is now a dirty, benighted, ill-provided, decaying place, with a population of about fifty-five thousand." He says elsewhere, "Cordova, poetic Cordova! when seen from afar with its drooping palms, the banners of the clime, its Moorish towers, walls, and pinnacles, appears beautiful as in the days of the luxurious, high-bred Abderrahman.... Alas for poor Cordova!"

But the Mosque remains still, though how defiled and degraded! Many of the portals have been walled up; the beautiful seat of the Caliph is filled with all kinds of church finery; the walls, once so delicately and richly carved, are hidden by tawdry decorations. You feel inclined to cry out vengeance against the despoilers of a temple which Solomon's could not have surpassed.

It is the most wonderful place, and one can understand what a grand religious conception the Moors must have had when inside this, their temple of temples. After all, the Mahomedans were much more tolerant and enlightened than the people they alternately ruled and served, and were Unitarians, *pur et simple*, praying to the universal God, in whose name never was raised a more fitting house of prayer.

To have seen the Mosque of Cordova forms an era in one's life. It is so vast, so solemn, so beautiful. You seem to be wandering at sunset time in a large and dusky forest, intersected by regular alleys of tall, stately palms. No matter in what direction you turn your face, northward, southward, eastward, westward, the same beautiful perspective meets your eye, file after file of marble and jasper columns supporting the double horse-shoe arch. Nothing can be more imposing, and at the same time graceful, than this arrangement of transverse aisles; and the interlaced arches, being delicately coloured in red and white, may not inaptly be compared to foliage of a palm-forest, flushed with the rays of the setting sun. If so impressive now, what must this place have been in the glorious days of Abderrahman, the Al-Raschid of Cordova, when the roofs blazed with arabesques of red and blue and "patines of bright gold;" the floors were covered with gorgeous carpets, and the aisles swarmed with thousands of worshippers in their bright Eastern dresses? The richest imagination cannot ever paint the scene, the readiest fancy cannot embellish it, and only those who have imbibed the rich colours of the East can close their eyes and dream of it. When the dream is over, cast your eyes along the long lines of columns, and you will see where the shoulders of spectators and worshippers of ages have left an enduring mark—a touching sight!—and then go into the once exquisite Maksura or Caliph's seat, and weep to see what becomes of beautiful things in Spain!

Words are not strong enough to condemn the

desecration of such a temple,—a temple worthy of the purest religion the world will ever know. Let the Catholic services be celebrated within its walls, let the priests preach from its altars, let the people kneel on its floors—but why, in heaven's name, should every exquisite relic of Moorish art, and every vestige of Moorish devotion, be ruthlessly destroyed? One marvels to see even the pillars and horse-shoe arches left intact—who knows for how long? And there are still some inlaid ceilings of thuya wood, and some fragments of arabesque stucco, as remarkable for richness of design and delicacy of work as any of the Alhambra. But to those who are curious in such things, I say—See them soon, or you will be too late. It is always a question of Now or Never in Spain.

It is curious that Cespedes, the Spanish Crichton, or, as some call him, the Spanish Michel-Angelo, wrote a learned dissertation, trying to prove that, where this glorious Mosque now stands, a temple once stood dedicated to Janus, erected by the Romans after the conquest of Spain. Cespedes was a native of Cordova (*hijo de Corduba*), and a man of whom she has every reason to be proud. He was a scholar, an antiquary, a poet, a painter, a critic. Look at his pictures "if ever you should go to Cordova."

When you have seen the Mosque you will have seen all that the Spaniards have left there. There were formerly Roman antiquities of no ordinary interest, aqueducts, an amphitheatre, and monuments, of which not a trace remains. Will it be believed that, in making the prisons of the Inquisition, some statues, mosaics, and inscriptions were found, all of which were covered again by the holy tribunal as being Pagan.* Of the Aladdin-like palaces of Abderrahman, there is not a vestige; mediæval Cordova, with its architecture, its arts, and its prosperity, is disappearing bit by bit, whilst, like some physical manifestation of energetic disease, a large and splendid Plaza for bull-fights has sprung up!

A melancholy Italian acted as *cicerone*, and carried us to a lovely Eastern garden, just

---

* Ford.

outside the town. Here were orange-trees bearing blossom and fruit, and the paler lemon, bosquets of myrtle and cistus making the air heavy with sweetness; clusters of gorgeous tropical flowers, crimson and yellow and purple; palm-trees glowing against the deep blue sky; ponds full of gold and silver fish, and everything lovely and gracious to both eye and senses.

Then we went to the market-place—a picturesque sight, for it was covered from end to end with heaps of the pretty hand-painted pottery of Andujar and Talavera. My friend was so enchanted with the taste displayed in this ware, both as to form and colour, that she bought a great quantity of it,—jugs, plates, cups, and basins, all shaped and coloured differently, and each piece costing no more than a few rials. This and lace from La Mancha—Don Quixote's country—was all we found worth buying at Cordova; for the leather-work was not nearly so elaborate, and much costlier, than that so plentiful in Algiers. The lace is made of coarse thread, but is very pretty, and is used plentifully in Andalusia for decorating sheets and pillow-cases. We could but notice the extreme civility of the humble sellers of pottery in the market-place, and the impertinent *nonchalance* of the smart shopman who sold us the lace. The former, a well-to-do Andalusian peasant-woman, could not take too much pains about pleasing us, carried us home to her little house, in order to show us her stock-in-trade, introduced us to her daughter, and smiled alike whether we approved or no. The shopmen puffed away at their cigars, laughed and talked among themselves whilst attending to their customers, cared little whether we bought or no, and greeted us in quite a familiar fashion when we came away. Certainly the Spaniards play at business in a most amateur style, and can never be accused, as we are, of being a nation of shopkeepers. The ladies laugh and talk with the shopmen over their purchases; and if we may believe Mesonero and other satirists of the day, many a rendezvous is made under the pretext of "shopping." You cannot take up a fashionable Spanish novel or play in which the ladies don't talk of assignations and shops as if the one belonged to the other; and whilst the scrupulous way in which young girls are chaperoned wherever they go, would seem to hint at some danger lurking in their favourite occupation.

Young Spanish ladies never walk out unattended, and whenever Englishwomen chose to do so, their deviation from social orthodoxy is severely commented upon. Spanish ladies too, I have read somewhere, when promenading the streets *en grande tenue*, are flattered by the admiration, expressed or implied, of passers-by! —a notion so opposed to our English sense of delicacy that it is entertained with difficulty. Yet the bearing of the pretty, dark-eyed ladies we saw about us, coquetting with the fan, sweeping the ground with long trains only suitable for a ball or presentation, raising their skirts with ungloved jewelled hands, so as to show their pretty feet, go far to support the notion. A well-dressed English lady does not think of her dress; one cannot help seeing that a well-dressed Madrilenian does. She is very attractive, notwithstanding.

I would not advise any one to hurry away

from Cordova, especially if he is an artist. The place is so picturesque in itself, and so full of poetic association, that a few days may well be devoted to it, especially in the beautiful autumn, when all kinds of glories are cast about hill, and tower, and river.

CHAPTER VII.

"THE SWEETEST MORSEL OF THE PENINSULA."—COB-WALLS OR THE HOUSE THAT CAIN BUILT.—PALMS.—THE GOOD WORKS OF THE SISTERS.—THE PRIESTS AND THE PEOPLE.—IS SPAIN UTOPIA?

THE journey from Cordova to Malaga lasts from six in the morning till five in the afternoon. You are, of course, aroused at four and carried off to the station at five; so that you are really on the way much longer. But the scenery of Andalusia is so varied and beautiful that you are almost sorry when the train reaches its destination.

Beautiful Andalusia! so quaintly called by a lover of it, "the sweetest morsel of the Peninsula." Who can forget or over-praise its voluptuous southern sky, its rich brown plains, its glistening white villages peeping amid groves of the cistus, the ilex, and the cork-tree, its green slopes crowned with Moorish towers and palaces, its delicious climate, its trickling streams, its sweet-smelling flowers?

The railway is new and carries one through a most astounding bit of country. After passing leagues of olive orchards, we found ourselves suddenly in a wholly different world. First came range after range of cold grey mountains, then perpendicular columns of limestone of gigantic size, evidently thrown up by volcanic action. These rocks and their counterparts have been admirably drawn by Gustave Doré in his splendid *Don Quixote*, and are quite awful in their height and barrenness.

The train went at a snail's pace right through the heart of the gorge, and during this part of the journey, most of the passengers got out and walked! I suppose the line was not quite safe, and indeed the soil is so light and sulphurous that it seems impossible ever to make it so. We kept our seats, however. What a slow journey it was! Sometimes we hardly seemed to move at all, and kept stopping at little signal stations so long that we read and wrote letters, worked, and sketched, as if at home in our own drawing-room.

The guards were most civil, as usual, and did their best to explain matters to us. The railway would go quickly enough by-and-by, they said, but the road was a difficult one to work, &c., &c. *Mañana, mañana* (to-morrow), everything will go quickly to-morrow, is the usual cry.

The villages of Andalusia are very picturesque, and remind you of the west of England, only here the foliage is richer, the skies are of a deeper blue, the landscape is wilder and more varied. Here the white cottages glisten, not amid groves of beech, elm, and willow, but amid the orange-tree, the ilex, and the olive; whilst the uncultivated plains, instead of being purple with heath and golden with gorse, are barren and sunburnt as the face of a gipsy, save where thickets of the cistus and the cork-tree break the dreary sameness.

But there is more than a fancied resemblance between the home of the Andalusian peasant and the Devonshire labourer. The walls of his cottage are constructed after precisely the same fashion, and of precisely the same materials—that primitive, cheap, durable mixture of earth and reeds, which, when whitewashed, tones down into a beautiful cream colour, surpassing the richest marble for softness and mellowness of tint. In beautiful Andalusia, "the poor cottager contents himself with cob for his walls, and thatch for his covering;" as quaintly says an old English writer, and what in England is called cob, with all its varieties of concrete cob, dry cob, rad and dab, &c., is only another variety of the tapia, or mud wall of the Arab and Moro-Andalusian. Of concrete cob indeed, that is, a mixture of lime, rough sand, pebbles, earth, and reeds rammed into cases, are formed not only the noble walls of Cordova and Granada, but the Moorish watch-towers or *atalayas*, that so grandly rise along the southern sea-coast. We might, if we were so disposed, trace this economical and excellent masonry down to Cain, the builder of the first city—at least, so says a learned authority on the subject.* And guided by the finger-

* "We shall trace cob," he says, "for a long period as peculiarly used by the Cainite branch. Cain built a city, ἣν οἰκοδομῶν

mark of learned authorities, we might follow its progress from east to west; for the simple art of cob-building links the cities and civilizations of the

πολιν. To build a city infers a considerable population, and a certain development of social life. As single houses must have preceded cities, Cain certainly had previously constructed a house for himself and his wife before the foundation of Enoch. It could not have been a log-house: he was unprovided with instruments of iron to fell or fashion timber, for the art of working metals was not discovered by Tubal Cain till afterwards. It could not have been of stone, or brick, or mortar: that implies a knowledge of chemistry. The use of bricks is first recorded at the Tower of Babel, where bitumen was used instead of mortar. Cain, we may fairly assume, must have built of mud or cob. . . . Mud was the obvious material to a tiller of the earth. Cain, an eater of corn, must have observed the increased cohesiveness of clay when mixed with stubble: he might have seen that exemplification in the nests of some birds in the air. Mud mixed with straw would make his cob, while fallen branches of trees and dried vegetable matter would furnish his roof. His cottage, as to its colour, most *certainly* resembled the red towers of the Alhambra, and the ferruginous cob of Exeter; for as the first house was built near the site of Eden, it must have been composed of the same earth from which the first man was made,—that red earth, βωλος ἐρυθρος, which gave the ancient original name of the Red Sea to the Persian Gulf,— that red dust from whence the first man was called Adam— Adham, the red, the earthy man."— *Quarterly Review*, No. CXVI. Art. Cob Walls.

ancient Egyptians and Phœnicians with those of the Devonshire peasant, the Andalusian, and the Moor of Barbary, of to-day. No one who travels through the south of Spain will fail to observe the picturesque aspect of its villages; and I have gone out of my way to notice this feature in them, because any relationship in the arts is interesting to a traveller. He will find traces of cob alike in India, in Mexico, in Greece, and in Italy; but nowhere is the original architecture of the Phœnicians more noteworthily copied than in the sunny plains of Andalusia.

After traversing this wilderness of limestone run mad, we glided into a warmer and lovelier zone. We fancied ourselves in Algeria. There were golden plumes of palm-trees waving against a deep blue sky; orange and lemon groves at the foot of bluer hills; hedges of aloe and wild cactus by the roadside; flowers and sunshine and sweetness everywhere. It was Sunday, too, and pretty it was to see the handsome Andalusian peasants in their gay dresses alight and descend at the different stations, with orange-branches, bearing golden fruit and glossy leaf, in their hands. Wherever we stopped there came Murillo-like children to the door, bringing glasses of fresh water, saying, " Agua fresca, agua fresca."

At the end of these beautiful Eastern pictures came Malaga, a large, white, dusty town, with a quiet blue sea at its feet, and above and around it the most wonderfully-coloured hills, purple, rose-colour, violet, blood-red, rainbow-hued in the sunset and colourless never.

We found Malaga, in spite of its delicious climate, its bright sea, its gorgeous hills, and its Eastern gardens, a disagreeable place. The streets always smelt of fish,—raw fish, cooked fish, fresh fish, dried fish, stale fish. The common people are dirty and unpleasant, a mongrel race, half-gipsy, half-bandit, with an evil look. The pavements are filthy, and all the time of our stay a sirocco was blowing, so that we were choked with dust wherever we went.

We stayed here several days nevertheless; and though we never liked Malaga, could not fail to be enchanted with the oriental look of the place. Just outside of the town were lovely gardens full of roses and geraniums in blossom, and here and there clusters of palms overspreading white-domed Moorish *algibe,* or wells ; whilst we drove for miles along a road hedged in by the beautiful African reed, so like gigantic corn, that is golden in the sunshine and black as the cypress at twilight.

The colouring of the mountains is most delicious, and in part makes up for the fishiness and filthiness of the streets. A ray of the setting sun turns the whole wild sierra into a pageantry of pink, deepest violet, crimson, and amber, and makes you long to be an artist in order to transfix the wonderful scene. Mountain and palm, city and tower and sea, seen through the medium of so rare an atmosphere, might well tempt an artist to linger here.

The English Consul was very kind to us, and from him we learned a good deal that was interesting about the place. He took us to the Protestant Cemetery—a beautifully kept garden covering a hill by the sea-side, from whence we had a lovely view. It is a sweet spot ; the graves lie in clusters around the chapel, and are half hidden by all kinds of tropic trees and flowers, the graceful pepper-tree, the orange, the lemon, the palmetto, the cistus, the lily; whilst above them stretch sunny slopes, newly planted with the vine and the fig. The soil is very red in colour and full of iron, which accounts for the beauty and the fertility of the landscape everywhere. I believe that for this boon of a burial-place, alike English and foreign Protestants are solely indebted to the father of the present Consul. Protestantism is an obnoxious weed in Catholic Spain, and all those unfortunate Protestants who died at Malaga before our Consul's intervention, were buried like dogs in holes dug along the sea-shore. Now, no matter what a man's faith and nation may be, if shut out of the Spanish burial-ground, he finds a resting-place here.

What gave us as much pleasure as anything in Malaga, was the sight of some orphanages, founded by a young, rich, and beautiful Spanish widow lady, who, having lost her husband and children by sudden deaths, devotes all her time and money to charitable works. The schools are under the direction of the Sisters of St. Vincent de Paul, and the letter of introduction we carried with us procured ready admittance. The Sisters who received us had beautiful faces, a little sad perhaps, but expressive of the utmost peace and piety. One was a girl of twenty, and she had the sweetest eyes, brown, soft, and shy, with a child's complexion, all pink and white, and a child's rosy mouth—though not a child's gaiety.

"But you are a Frenchwoman, *ma sœur*," we said; "and you too!" we added, turning to the elder sister. "How is this? Are there not Spanish women enough to work for their own poor and fatherless?"

The elder sister shook her head.

"There are plenty of good Spanish women devoted to charity," she answered, "but they seem wanting in energy and the love of organisation. They are content to serve, but have no desire to act and to travel. Now, we go to the uttermost ends of the earth and like it."

"Yes; you see plenty of the world, *ma sœur*, you are always busy on good works. It is an enviable lot."

She smiled, part pleased, part sad.

"We are content if we can do a little in the service of the Virgin and the blessed Saviour; but, alas! how little!"

"Do not say that, *ma sœur*. We who stand outside the Church are made better for your example of self-denial and benevolence."

"Ah! you are Protestants, of course. Many come here to see the children at work."

We now made the round of the school-rooms and *ateliers*, where we found children divided according to age. The little ones, from three to five, were seated on tiers of benches, as in our infant-schools, and were at lessons under the superintendence of a sweet-looking young woman, also a native of France. The system seemed admirable. The teacher held up a letter, and instantaneously every little hand waved, and every little mouth opened to say, "I see an A," "I see a B," "I see a C," and so on, till the whole alphabet had been gone through. Their little lessons in spelling and arithmetic were gone through on the same plan, every response being accompanied by a gesture. The children seemed thoroughly to enjoy the lesson, and no wonder. It was as good as a game of gymnastics to them. I am sure this system is the only desirable one to pursue with very young children, who are like young animals, always wanting to frisk about. Every one who has had anything to do with village schools knows how difficult it is for the mistress to keep the little ones still, and how they are scolded, sent to the corner, and kept over hours for sinning in this respect. But the Sisters have no troubles of this kind, and by keeping body and mind alike active no time or temper is wasted on either side.

From the infant-school we went into the class-room and *ateliers* of the elder girls, and examined some very beautiful needlework, thread-lace, and embroidery, some completed and ready for sale, others in process. These children are all taken from the lowest classes; their work is sold and the proceeds set apart for them till such a time as they need a dowry, or outfit for service. Each child is, therefore, laying up a little nest-egg for herself, and is, at the same time, acquiring a profitable and womanly handicraft, and, what is even more important, a good moral training.

In a town like Malaga, where the lower ranks have been leavened with the yeast of brigandage, such an influence must be invaluable. I do not remember the average number of little scholars who come daily to be fed and taught by the Sisters of St. Vincent de Paul, but it is a large one.

What Malaga must be in the summer-time I have no idea, not having lived in tropical climates; but whilst we were there, in the last week of November, the heat was very trying. The much-vaunted Alameda, which is really a pretty walk, was unbearable on account of the wind, and sun, and dust; and it was not till we had got a mile out of the town that the air was fresh and pure. There are some charming country-houses with gardens, around Malaga, but it is only within the last half-dozen years that the proprietors have been able to use or let them. The banditti ruled the country with a rod of iron; land was comparatively worthless; travelling unsafe. As late as 1857 murder and assassination were so common in the streets of Malaga that a resident* wrote home, " The country is in a miserable state. The streets are not safe for a single person late at night. Murder is not thought much more of here than pocket-picking in England."

* Rev. James Meyrick.

Later, however, government has been working with a will to put down the brigands, and with such success that purchasing land is become a profitable speculation. People may now build country-houses, plant groves, and vineyards in safety. It is a pity there is no good hotel in the suburbs, for I think few invalids could support the bad smells and heat of the town.

Besides the palms and the purple hills, Malaga possesses superb vineyards. Who does not associate the very name of the place with raisins and sweet wine? And those who want to know what a Spanish vintage is, should come here in the early autumn. Wherever we went, we came in contact with mules heavily laden with boxes of raisins, of which I believe a million are exported every year; but the vintage was over, and after a week we were ready to go into Granada. Whilst we are yet in Catholic Spain (for who thinks of anything but the Moors at Granada?) let me recur to a very important subject. Of course, the passing traveller through Spain has very little opportunity of judging such important questions as the practical working of the Church. But it is a question of the deepest interest, and cannot fail to rise in an earnest mind again and again. Spain is the country of all others which Romanists will be inclined to regard as the faithful child of the only true Church. Is she indeed as faithful as tradition warrants—as love takes on credence? Alas! I fear the most devoted Catholic would not be able to say, yes. The first thing that strikes you on coming into the country is the contemptuous tone taken by all classes when speaking of the priests. What wonder, indeed? The priesthood is recruited from the lowest ranks; the priest is uneducated, ill-paid, often reputed to be immoral, always without dignity. Confessional is a dead letter. Infidelity is found among the rich; immorality among the poor. Wherever we went, we noticed the coarse, dull faces of the priests, and the irreverence of the people towards them. Of course there are exceptions, but, as a rule, the priest is held in slight esteem, whether deserving or no. "Not even the courtesy of Spaniards can make them behave decently to a priest," says a candid and careful writer, who spent several years in Spain, and published some admirable letters on the practical working of the Church there.* From these letters, and my own observations, I have come to the painful conclusion that good Romanists will find Spain far from being the orthodox Utopia of their imagination. The churches are falling into ruin, the clergy are miserably paid, partly by a tax, partly by fees, a parish priest receiving about £80 a year, a *beneficiado*, or curate, about £40. Confessional and Communion are neglected by the young; and, where orthodoxy exists, it goes hand in hand with the deepest ignorance. Mariolatry is carried to the highest pitch, and the most absurd stories of modern miracles are believed in, and the Scriptures are a sealed book. In a little volume called the *Manual of the Seminarista*, is a chapter on the Scriptures which, the author states, " boys and women are not to have, because their natural simplicity is often mixed with ignorance and presumption, and leads them into heresies." " Never shall I forget," says the author first quoted, " the eagerness with which Don F—— borrowed my Spanish Testament when he found it was what he

* Rev. J. Meyrick, *Church of Spain*.

called *puro.* "We only get garbled scraps here," he said; and he gives some most interesting and valuable letters from a Spanish priest to an English clergyman, wherein occur the following passages: "As you well know, the true and genuine gospel of Christ cannot be preached in Spain, but the gospel of the Pope, which is a very different thing indeed from that. Here there is not the Spirit, for where the Spirit is there is liberty. Our very bishops have nothing in common with the Apostles: they do not preach the Word—they do not instruct the people. All they do is for hire; they accommodate everything to their sensual conceptions and earthly desires ... The Bishop of —— has never preached the word of God, and so ignorant is he that he knows nothing except the ceremonies, and this is all that he requires in a priest. At the last synod for providing *curas* (priests) he forbade the theologians, as is the old custom, to test the candidates' sufficiency by theological questions and dissertations! The Spaniards, having all these things before their eyes, laugh at the mission of the Christian priesthood, are losing their faith and morals, and sinking into atheism .... It cannot be denied that the Spaniards of the present day are generally opposed to Roman practices, and rather agree with you and me in thinking and doing than with them; such is the force of reason and truth. However, while they are giving up the errors of Romanism, they have no rule of faith and morality to embrace, and, led as by a blind impulse, each has prescribed a liberal and irregular belief for himself, which sometimes he follows and sometimes relinquishes . . . . Will you, then, associate yourselves together for the work of the Gospel in these regions? Will you, in your charity, lead this people to the true faith of Christ? Will you recall them from atheism or indifferentism to the Church of God? Establish evangelical missions, and support them with your pious alms. The Romanists labour night and day to propagate their errors; they send their fanatical missionaries to go round the world, and all sorts of sectaries run eagerly to the work. But ye, who profess the true faith of Christ, will ye leave a thirsty people to perish, and give them naught out of your abundance when they ask?" These extracts, short as they are, throw floods of light upon the present state of religious feeling in Spain. I remember that we saw, with some surprise, a translation of Renan's *Vie de Jésus* in a bookseller's shop at Madrid, and heard two young men discuss it over their purchases with no few heresies expressed or implied. I suppose infidelity is a lesser crime than Protestantism in Catholic Spain. Protestantism is, in fact, entirely forbidden. Foreigners, being Protestants, are allowed to meet together for religious purposes at the office or house of their respective Consuls; but any Spaniard found among the congregation would be liable to some punishment. In 1850, the Rev. James Meyrick was assured by a canon of Cordova Cathedral that, according to the existing law of Spain, any Spaniard departing from the Romish doctrine is liable to capital punishment, though he added that he thought no government would now attempt to enforce that law. Any Protestant reading the service of the Protestant Church, excepting under the protection of his flag, would, with his congregation, be liable to fines, imprisonment, or dismissal from the country.

A few years ago it was necessary to have a certificate of confession before holding any office under the government, and the certificates were bought and sold for tenpence! Of course the greatest ignorance exists regarding the Scriptures. People confound the legends of modern times with the sacred history, and have as much faith in the one as the other. Every one has read Borrow's extraordinary adventures in Spain, and will recall the story of the Alcalde, who after discoursing learnedly about Bentham, Lope de Vega, and Plato, took up the New Testament and asked, "What book is this?" Upon Borrow answering him he said, "Ha, ha! how very singular!—yes, I remember. I have heard that the English highly prize this eccentric book. How very singular that the countrymen of the great Bentham should set any value upon that old monkish book!" Mariolatry is carried to the same excess one sees in Italy. Ford, in his *Gatherings*, gives a striking instance of this in describing the execution of the robber Veneno. "The criminal exclaimed *Viva la religion! Viva el rey! Viva el nombre de Jesus!* All of which met no echo from those who heard him. His dying cry was, *Viva la Virgen Santisima!* At these words the devotion to the goddess of

Spain broke forth in one general acclamation, *Viva la Santisima!*"

In the reign of Charles III., 1759-1780, a law was enacted, requiring a declaration upon oath of a firm belief in the Immaculate Conception, from everybody taking his degree at the university, or being admitted into any corporation, civil or religious, or even into a mechanic's guild. The Virgin's altars, images, robes and jewels, are gorgeous beyond description. At her name both priest and congregation made reverence. It is to her altars that the people flock. It is she who is represented as the guide and ruler of the Church, and the intercessor between God and man. To her are addressed most of the hymns and prayers by which indulgences are obtained. There is one hymn in a little book of prayers called the *Novena*, the repetition of which will procure more indulgence than a year of rigorous penances. This indulgence clears you from penance, or the indefinite consequences of neglected penance in purgatory; and if by a certain number of litanies, rosaries, and hymns, so much indulgence is gained, who would fast or otherwise do penance?

One cannot but lament this state of things, and equally lamentable is the condition of the priests and the position of the priesthood. There are, doubtless, many good and devout men in their ranks, but, as a body, they have lost caste and influence. When the friars were all ejected from the monasteries, they were weighed in the balance and found wanting; and friars and priests alike suffer still from a tide of antagonistic opinion. "No one knows, and no one will know until a revolution takes place," said a Spaniard to me, "how the priests are disliked." We ourselves noticed on several occasions a very low type of face among the priests with whom we came in contact, and their appearance is slatternly and often dirty in the extreme. These circumstances are easily accounted for when one reads of the way in which the army of the church is recruited. Most of the ejected friars were sons of peasants; and such a prejudice exists against taking holy orders, that very few parents of any social standing care to dedicate their sons to a profession so poor and so despised. It is true that a begging student of Salamanca may become a bishop, but that is the exceptionable case, the usual fate of a Spanish priest is to end his days a parish *cura* with an income of £40 a-year. I am sorry to say that the moral character of the clergy stands low.

It is pleasant to turn from such unsatisfactory prospects to the Sisters and their good works. Their predecessors had also their share of suffering. At the same time that the Government turned out the friars, many rich convents were confiscated too. There were three at Malaga that shared this fate. The nuns had entered with a dowry of from £120 to £400, which the abbess had spent on lands. They were living in the utmost comfort, each with her own apartments and servant. On a sudden, all was taken, and they were thrust out of their paradise as naked and helpless as Adam and Eve. Most of them had no home to go to, and gladly procured the humblest employment; some, it is said, perished of want. The worst of all was that the tide of public feeling had set so strongly against them, that they suffered torments of fear. No wonder that the priests were hated, for the memory of the Inquisition was still fresh, but the poor nuns had led harmless lives, often charitable ones, nursing the sick, and teaching the ignorant.*

There is no doubt that the ill-judged favour of royalty does more than anything else to fan the flames of popular dislike towards both priest and nun. Who is the Père Claret, the Queen's confessor? An adventurer, who has been alternately soldier, ecclesiastic, author, missionary, and who formerly gained a certain notoriety for having written a coarse book. Who is the Sœur Patrocinio, abbess of the convent of St. Pascual d'Aranjuez? An intriguing impostor, once condemned by the public tribunal for having pretended to the miraculous possession of the Stigmata, or wounds of Christ.

Alas! I think every impartial traveller in Catholic Spain must conclude his observations in the words of Pugin:—"*Pleasant meadows, happy peasants, all holy monks, all holy priests, holy everybody. Such charity and such unity where every man was a Catholic. I once believed in this Utopia myself, but when tested by stern facts, it all melts away like a dream.*"

* Rev. J. Meyrick.

CHAPTER VIII.

"A BOAT, A BOAT, MY KINGDOM FOR A BOAT!"—THE VICTIMS OF A TUNNY FISH.—SENOR BENSAKEN SPEAKS HIS MIND, AND WE ARE REPROVED.—RUNNING WATERS.—HOWLINGS OF TARSHISH. —PEPA'S FAMILY.

WE had another amusing instance of Spanish *nonchalance* at Malaga. The original plan of our journey was this:—to see the galleries of Madrid, the Moorish antiquities of Cordova, Seville, and Granada, and from the south of Spain cross over to Oran, and visit the beautiful old city of Tclemcen, the Granada of the West. But to get to Oran it was necessary to obtain information about boats, and this seemed an undertaking simply impossible. We ran hither and thither to the different steam-boat offices; we telegraphed to head-quarters at Gibraltar; we wrote dozens of letters of inquiry; we spent time, money, and patience; all availed nothing. Sometimes a glimpse of something like hope was vouchsafed to us. There was a weekly boat to Algeciras. There was a fortnightly boat from Gibraltar to Oran; there was a surfeit of boats one day, the next none at all. We were by turns advised to trust to the Algeciras boat, the Gibraltar boat, the Cadiz boat, till we came to the disheartening conclusion that we must give up Tclemcen altogether. No two statements ever agreed, and in this state of uncertainty we went off to Granada.

At six o'clock in the afternoon the diligence was to start, a great cumbersome vehicle divided into three compartments—berlina, coupé, and rotunda, and drawn by nine splendid mules in gay harness. We had taken the precaution to engage the berlina to ourselves,—a precaution I should earnestly recommend to all travellers who visit Spain before the completion of the railways brings back another age of gold. The berlina is a small compartment containing three seats and numerous little bags and hooks for the stowage of small baggage; it is somewhat narrow, it is true, and an imprisonment of fifteen hours within such a compass, not a pleasant ordeal to go through. But what is that to the inconveniences of the rotunda, where you are crowded and cramped so that you cannot stir a limb, where you are stifled with smoke and deafened with the noise of voices, where you are poisoned by foul air and bad smells, and where you are subject to tyranny a thousand times worse than that of fleas? We had been forewarned of these things in time, and were thus enabled to perform the wearisome night-journey to Granada without too much fatigue.

The first part of it was amusing enough. We drove out of the town with a tremendous dash; and as we had a coachman, a postilion, and a runner to urge the mules on, no wonder that we got on very fast. The journey was all up-hill, and the diligence was heavily laden; but the mules seemed so anxious to go fast that one might have fancied a pack of wolves was at their heels. The runner had a very bad time of it. He seemed to know every mule by name, and made the most extraordinary noises to urge his beasts on. Every now and then he sprang on to the step and rested awhile; then, on a sudden, just as the mules were slackening their pace a little, he would jump to the ground, crack his whip, and utter the most diabolical sounds.

The night was starlight, and we were able to see something of the wild country through which we passed. At regular intervals we came upon a couple of *guardia civile*, or gendarmes, standing on each side of the road. They were motionless as statues and looked very brigand-like in their fierce sombreros, hanging cloaks, and tight-fitting gaiters. One of these *guardia civile*, well-armed, always accompanies the diligence, though the road is considered safe. Our escort was a thin, cadaverous-looking, but soldierly man, who alighted whenever we changed horses, to smoke a cigarette and drink a cup of chocolate, or glass of water. Spaniards seem to live on cigarettes and chocolate.

At five o'clock in the morning we stopped at a posada for nearly an hour, and very refreshing it was to stretch one's limbs and breathe the cool mountain air. The posada was an enormous rambling old place, but quiet and clean. The landlord showed us, with other travellers, into a room with a little fire, and very civilly promised

M

us chocolate. There were two Englishmen among the rest who bitterly complained of the coupé. "Think of it," they said, "we took the coupé to ourselves, and have had such horrid company all the way,—a big, strong-smelling, dried tunny-fish!"

"Perhaps it will be taken out here," I said, consolingly.

They shrugged their shoulders in a very low-spirited fashion and one replied despairingly,—

"It's ticketed to Granada, so there's no chance for us. Five hours longer of it! It's enough to drive one mad."

It was certainly enough to drive one into a very evil temper. The smell of salted tunny-fish is nearly as bad as anything in the way of smells can be, and reminds one of those odious combinations with which clever chemists once proposed to supersede shot and shell in driving away one's enemies. The victims in this instance were very long-suffering, and seemed to forget their troubles in a cigarette. They, too, ordered chocolate, but, like ourselves, had to wait for it.

At the last moment, just as the diligence was

An Accident.

ready to start, came cakes and chocolate, and after hastily swallowing a little of both, we entered our berlina. Here another amusing scene occurred. At the tail-end of the last moment, such packages as were addressed to Loja, the name of our halting-place, had to be brought from the roof to the diligence. Amongst others, was a light deal-box, which, by some mismanagement or other, fell with an awful crash into the gutter! Out came, as if by magic, all the paraphernalia of some poor little maiden's wardrobe and belongings: mantilla, gloves, dresses, slippers, needle-work, chocolate-boxes, love-letters tied up with ribbon, missal, rosary,—all lay sucking up the mire in inextricable confusion. Driver, postilion, landlord, and gendarme, stood still, looking overwhelmed and hopeless. After some minutes the driver picked up a glove, the postilion a shoe, the landlord a love-letter, the gendarme a thimble. Then, as if by mutual consent, they slowly and patiently rescued the miry treasures, stopping now and then to sigh over the ruinous condition of each. It was a very humble little outfit, doubtless of some nursemaid or milliner's apprentice, which made the accident all the more deplorable, and I daresay many of those muddy spots were washed out by tears alone. No one grumbled at the delay, and no one seemed to think that the reason of it was not a legitimate one. How unlike our English promptitude and bustle! It was quite touching to see the concern of the stately gendarme when he took up a neck-ribbon the beauty of which was gone for ever. "*La pobrecita! La pobrecita!* (Poor little thing! poor little thing!) she'll never be able to wear that again," he ejaculated.

When everything had been replaced in the broken box, we went on. Now came the tiresome part of the journey. The early morning air was very cold, the road monotonous, and the berlina seemed to become narrower and more suffocating every league we went.

At last we reached Granada. At first sight we were disappointed with the aspect of the place; and indeed Cordova and Toledo are infinitely more impressive as approached by the ordinary road, but afterwards our preconceived ideas were a hundred-fold realised.

Arrival.

Crowds of beggars, the halt, the lame, and the blind, surrounded the diligence, and it was with some difficulty we got out. Some of the beggars were of loathsome appearance, victims of horrible disease and depravity, and all were terribly importunate. Amongst the crowd was a tall, thin, poor-looking old man, wrapped in a shabby Spanish cloak, who came up to us at once and said in excellent English, "How much baggage have you, ladies?" and on our replying, busied himself with it, and with us, in a way that seemed a little unwarrantable. Commissionnaires and guides stick to you like leeches, and we had determined to employ Bensaken, the well-known cicerone of Ford, of Owen Jones, and of hundreds of travellers. This old man looked more like a beggar than anything else, and, but for his proud manner, I think I should have bribed him with a few cuartos to go away. As it was, I sent a little lad after a fiacre, and managed my luggage myself, not feeling inclined to accept anonymous services, after having heard such golden reports of Emmanuel Bensaken. Our old friend, however, seated himself on the box, and not thinking it worth while to deprive him of the pleasure of the drive, we said nothing, and drove off.

Never was a hotel so enchantingly situated as the Hotel Ortiz, to which we had been recommended.

The Hotel Ortiz stands in the Alhambra gardens. The windows let in golden sunshine, and you look over bright yellow avenues of elms and panoramic views of plain and mountain. The Alhambra is quite near. Here you have a glimpse of battlement, superb in colour and outline, there a tower. The air is light, and warm, and balmy. Everybody has a pleasant smile and a brisk air, and goes about singing. The rooms are sunny, and have charming views, and the Alhambra is close by! It seems too good to be true.

After a bath and some excellent tea and bread and butter, the first we had tasted in Spain, and a little rest, we asked for Señor Bensaken.

Señor Bensaken was in the house, and would wait upon the Señoras at once, was the reply. After waiting an hour, again we asked for Bensaken. "Has he not been?" was the surprised answer. "We sent him to you long ago." But no Bensaken appeared, and as it was now late in the afternoon, we gave up all idea of seeing the Alhambra that day, and strolled into the gardens instead.

I should say there is no lovelier time than autumn for these beautiful avenues of tall elms, these shelving banks and trickling streams. The melancholy of the season harmonizes with the melancholy of this place; and the setting suns bestow a blood-red pomp, as of a battle-field, upon the glorious plain of the Vega.

The great charm of the Alhambra gardens is the constant purling and plashing of water. You never lose sight or sound of this purling and plashing of melted snow charmed from cool haunts in the Sierra Nevada, and both sight and sound grow upon you like sweet music. The flower-beds, once so carefully kept, are now sadly neglected, but the borders of myrtle and violets are lovely in neglect, and the orange and lemon trees bear blossom and fruit as of old. We lingered till sunset, when the old towers and the yellow forest of elm-trees, were burnished to the hue of brightly-polished copper, and the plain below was flecked with deep shadows, black and purple, and golden.

Beyond rose the blue and grey mountains of the Sierra Nevada, their crests shining with the silvery brightness of everlasting snow, in a belt of rosy sky. It was a scene of enchantment.

When we returned to our hotel, we were informed that Bensaken awaited us in the corridor, or *salle à manger;* what was our surprise to find Bensaken, the renowned guide, and our old friend in the threadbare cloak, one and the same person!

"Why, Señor Bensaken," we said, "you should have introduced yourself to us at first. We had no idea it was you, or we should have engaged you as guide on the spot."

The old man was evidently much offended with us.

"Señora," he said, "it is not my habit to push myself in where I am not wanted, and you preferred to employ that Spanish boy. *Corriente!* you had to please yourselves."

"But," we urged, "how could we know that you were Señor Bensaken? Why did you not give us your card? We had come to Granada with the intention of employing no other guide but Bensaken. We sent for you this afternoon, and you did not come." He had evidently stayed away out of displeasure, and we found it very difficult to heal the sore of which we felt so innocent. At last, growing a little impatient, we said sharply,—

" Señor Bensaken, it is really through your own stupidity, and no fault of ours, that this mistake occurred. If you are willing to act as guide to us, we are willing to engage you, and let the matter end."

The matter did end, and Señor Bensaken became our cicerone. He is a very old man, stiff in manner, aristocratic in appearance, and very entertaining when the mood takes him; full of stories of the great men he has known, Longfellow, Irving, and others. His English is wonderfully elegant, and he speaks several European languages, besides Arabic. But travellers must make haste to Granada who wish to secure his services, for he is in the sere and yellow leaf, and he coughs terribly.

The next day being Sunday, the Alhambra was not open, so we went to see the Cathedral and the Carthusian Convent. The Convent is very rich in inlaid doors and altars of silver, ebony, and tortoise-shell, and is curious in many respects. On the cloister walls are some paintings that Spanish guides show English tourists with sly looks. They represent the persecutions of the English Carthusians by Henry VIII., and one finds the same subject illustrated in other Carthusian convents, which is but natural. Lutheran bigotry still appears to the orthodox Spaniard as dreadful as it then was. The youthful Spanish mind is as vigorously infused with a hatred and fear of heresy as ever, and in the history of Spain used for schools and institutions of the second instruction *(Los Institutos y Colegios de segunda enseñanza)* occur such passages as these :—

"Por los Paises Bajos prosperaban,
Los odiosos errores de Lutero."

(The odious errors of Luther were prospering in the Low Countries.)

There is a charming view from the terrace of the convent, which, perhaps, repays the traveller for his trouble more than anything to be seen within its walls. The Cathedral every one will naturally visit, on account of the superb monuments of Ferdinand and Isabella. Mass was going on when we entered, and we could not but notice the terribly irreverent behaviour of the congregation, the choristers, and acolytes. They had, some of them, vicious faces, and all stared about and whispered to each other, and behaved as if they were at a bull-fight.

In the afternoon we drove on the Alameda, very gay at this hour, with a band playing, and ladies promenading, as a Spanish author says, in all their "atractivos;" officers darting past on pretty Andalusian horses, and all the world of Granada out for a holiday.

Granada is very conservative,—*Españolisimo* still to the backbone, which is rather trying to a traveller's patience. In spite of the annual influx of foreigners, a foreigner is still stared at and commented on. If you sit down to make a sketch, you are sure to have an obtrusive crowd around you, and I don't think English ladies could walk with comfort in the town unless accompanied by a guide. At least, we were advised not to try it. It is not that the common people are malicious, but they are so childishly astonished at the sight of strangers, that you feel as if you were a bear being led through a country-town on fair day. Every one has something to say about the bear.

Some of the people were, nevertheless, delightful, the family at the Ortiz, for example. The father acted as cook, the mother as house-keeper, the daughters as chambermaids, and the son as waiter. All were kindly, intelligent, and as gay as larks from morning till night. There was always singing in the house and garden, the same monotonous Arab singing we used to hear at Toledo and Cordova, but here, in sprightly Andalusia, it was infinitely improved upon. The daughters of the house were very pretty, with bright eyes, small regular features, elegant little figures, and great vivacity of expression. One was married, and had a dear little girl, about three, who used to greet us with an English "good morning!" she had learned somewhere. When their work was done, and it seemed done very early in the day, the sisters used to sit on the doorsteps, a friend or two would join them, and what with gossip, needle-work, and singing, they had a merry time of it.

The hotel was quite a little paradise of pleasantness and comfort. From every window were long views of the Alhambra walls and garden; there were very few visitors excepting ourselves, so that we had the *salle à manger* to ourselves, and the people were so kind and careful of our comfort that we could willingly have stayed a month.

Though we were already in December the weather was perfect, soft, golden, and balmy. We were glad of a little wood fire at night, but could have roamed about all day without our bonnets on. Roses and geraniums blossomed in the garden; and, whenever we walked out, little Murillo-like boys offered us bunches of violets.

Before entering the charmed precincts of the Alhambra I must mention a horrifying scene we witnessed just outside our windows. It was a pauper's funeral. We were warned of its approach by the sound of loud talking and laughter, and, on looking out, saw a wretched coffin borne by four men, smoking cigarettes, followed by a few lookers-on, all appearing equally unconcerned, and preceded by two or three men, who were, I suppose, the mourners, bearing lighted candles in their hands. There was no priest, no pall, no semblance of decency, and by-and-by our disgust was increased to the last pitch by the bearers setting the coffin on the bank, and leaning on it to rest themselves!

There is no sort of respect for death in Spain. The body of the pauper is carried to the cemetery in a coffin that belongs to the parish, and is thrust sometimes almost naked into a hole. The priests do not perform burial-service except for those who can afford to pay for it; they read a short service over the body in the church; and when once that ceremony is over, there is no more regard shown for the dead than for the slaughtered horse at a bull-fight. It is horrible.

CHAPTER IX.

DAYS IN THE ALHAMBRA.—THE GRANDEUR WITHOUT AND THE BEAUTY WITHIN.—" CIELED WITH CEDAR, AND PAINTED WITH VERMILION."—AZULEJOS AND ARTESONADOS.—MR. OWEN JONES' HANDBOOK.

THERE is no place in the world like the Alhambra, so graceful, so perfect, so sad. No words can describe it, no pencil can portray it; it remains apart in the heart and fancy, like some second, more golden youth, that has come for a brief season, and made us happy and passed away.

The gardens are bordered with violets and myrtle, and shadowy with orange and lemon trees; the marble floors, the dried fountain, the slender alabaster columns, the gorgeous ceilings, the walls covered with delicate arabesques and verses, the airy courts, the sunny fish-ponds, the luxurious baths, the silence and desolation that have fallen over all, are indeed indescribable, and grow upon one like the graces of a most musical poem.

It is a fairy tale for men and women of all countries and religions—a realization of beauty, the most inconceivable and the most intoxicating—a sweet and subtle embodiment of Eastern thought and art. The Alhambra is so ruined as a whole, and yet so perfect in parts, so bare here, so rich in colour there, so desolate and yet so haunted by voices, that it reminds one most, I think, of beautiful antique jewellery. Some of the jewels have dropped out, the gold is tarnished, the clasp is broken, the crown is bent, but gaze a little while, and all becomes as it once was. Pearl and amethyst, emerald and opal, blaze out on some lovely throat, a golden clasp is wound on some round white arm, and a crown shines on some golden head, perhaps of a goddess, perhaps of a woman. Nothing is lost, or changed, or dead.

One doesn't know what to admire most in this small but exquisite realm of enchantment. Like children at a fair, who clap their hands and

laugh for joy at every new toy, crying out,—
" This is best! no, this! no, this!" we passed from
court to court, and hall to hall, declaring each
to rival each as we went along. At one time
I held that the court of Lindaraja bore the palm,
at another the Alberca; but each is so perfect
in its way that it is almost impossible to have
preference for any. The view of the Alberca,
or fish-pond court, is very sweet on a sunny day.
We first saw it when the sunlight were playing
on the water, and the rainbow-coloured reflexion
of it on the delicate alabaster colums was magical.
But all is magical—the Court of Lions, the Baths,
the Hall of Ambassadors, the Mezquita, the Hall
of the Two Sisters; and one could weep at the
desecration that has done its best to ruin them.

What never ceases to surprise you is the
richness and the delicate, one might almost say,
effeminate finish and elaborateness of every part.
The walls are covered with coloured *faïence* and
arabesques; the ceilings are either of inlaid pine
or cedar wood, and hollowed after the fashion
of stalactite caves; the floors are of polished white
marble, the palm-like columns, of alabaster and

fountains abound everywhere. There is nothing to add and nothing to take away from this Palace of Aladdin; and as you learn to know the place, you love it, and marvel at it more and more. But if it is a Palace of Aladdin now, what must it have been when the fountains were shedding floods of pearl in the sunlight; when all the courts were filled with perfume of myrtle, of oleander, and of orange-blossom; when the glistening white floors were partly hidden by gorgeous carpets; when the delicate columns were covered with gold, and the fretted domes blazed with colour, orange, purple, and red; when the Caliph administered justice, surrounded by his courtiers, a second Solomon with more than Solomon's glory; when the Alberca Court rang with the merry voices of Moorish girls, who bathed, and played, and told each other love-stories all day long; when every hall echoed with voices, and was bright with the rich Oriental dresses, what must it have been indeed? Only the poets and chroniclers of the time can tell us; but their name is Legion, for never did the sun of patronage shine brighter than under the Ommeyad dynasty, and the glories and disasters of beautiful Granada formed a favourite theme of both poet and poetess.

The Alhambra is not understood in a day. At first sight you are apt to be disappointed. The courts are smaller than you thought, or they seem over-laden with ornament, or they want breadth here, loftiness there; but this is only the captiousness of ignorance. Like a beautiful, capricious child, who tries you and torments you one moment, and the next is all sweetness and grace, and only in need of caresses, the Alhambra must be taken on trust; and when you have seen it as we saw it, in the pearly light of early morning, in the blaze of noon-day sun, in the dusky twilight, in the silvery night, you will come away, filled with the joy that is born of beauty, and thank the happy chance that led your steps to Granada. The outer walls and towers are very grand; but to enjoy their grandeur you must lose sight of the Palace of Charles V., the rankest toad-stool that ever grew up amid sweet summer flowers.

We had come to Gránada in the season of sunsets, and what sunsets they were! Then the long lines of broken wall, ordinarily of that rich yellow colour, with which the pipe stains white marble, were flushed into deepest crimson, the faded elms were aglow with rosy light, the whole world seemed floating in golden mist. Or if we lost sight of the walls, and turned our faces westward, we looked across a broad purple plain, bounded by the snow-tipped Sierra, behind which the sun was setting in an unutterable splendour of colour and light. Another moment, and the blaze was gone; pink clouds, like rose-leaves, floated about the sky and disappeared slowly, one by one, and, last of all, came the bluish-grey twilight, and myriads of large southern stars.

One grows so rooted to the place, for sake of its many-sided beauty,—beauty of art, of atmosphere, of everything, that one never wishes to leave it. That is to say, if one were an intellectual being one would never wish to leave it; but the material part of every poor person and every Protestant must make the thought of dying at Granada simply horrible. I never felt such a distaste for Catholic Spain, and such a respect for Mahomedan Spain, as here. The Moors made Granada the paradise we find it, and it was an evil hour for the civilised world when their enlightened rule came to an end. Everything good in Granada is Moorish; instead of arts, philosophy, toleration, charity, and wealth, came ignorance, the Inquisition, superstition, misery, pauperism.

But let us forget these things and give our time and thoughts to the Alhambra. It is quite marvellous that such a creation—what other name can one use in speaking of the Alhambra?—should have been the work of the last period of Mahomedan glory. Like some flower, the last and loveliest of an Indian summer, it only reached maturity when the sun, that had ripened it, was on the wane; and hardly had the petals opened one by one when they were nipped by frost and wind. Everything that contempt and malice, and it must be admitted also earthquakes, could do, was done to despoil the fairy palace of the Moors, and the only marvel is, that anything remains to show what it once was. This mixture of beauty and desolation on every side reminds one of Heidelberg; only that Heidelberg is less perfect and less melancholy, since with its prosperity, the civilisation that had called it into existence did not pass away:

Descriptions, however poetic or minute, photographs, water-colour drawings, fail to give one a complete idea of the Alhambra. A single visit disappoints all preconceived expectation. To know it and value it for what it is, it must be seen again and again, and studied in every part; and to appreciate it according to its real worth, requires real knowledge of Moorish art and sympathy with its deep religious feeling.

"The architecture of the Arabs," says Mr. Owen Jones, "is essentially religious, and the offspring of the Koran, as Gothic architecture is of the Bible. And this truth must always be held in the traveller's remembrance. Indeed, it is impossible to understand any of the great works of the Moors without having read the Koran, their reverence for which is testified in the numerous texts from it with which they adorned their walls. In the Alhambra these sacred writings have been most gorgeously and elaborately inscribed; and what Arabic scholars consider as a labour of love, with no omission of vowel or grammatical sign. In writing ordinary Arabic the vowels are treated as if they were women and are kept out of sight, but as the Koran admits women to Paradise, so Art admits the inferior letters into his service."*

The life of the East is so full of charm, that it is grateful alike to the heart and fancy to find in Arab architecture a transcript of it. Who can doubt that the graceful columns were suggested by the still more graceful palm, the light colonnade by the airy tent, the arabesques of colour and gold, by the silk stuff of Damascus? And the Alhambra itself, so gorgeous within, so unadorned and warlike and well defended without, may be called an embodiment of the spirit of the Koran, which is at

* I think the only book useful to all but the student who goes to Gayangos, Pranzes, and the great work of Owen Jones, is the last-named gentleman's *Hand-book to the Alhambra, Crystal Palace*. Of course everyone will carry his Ford; but, with regard to the Alhambra, Mr. Owen Jones's pamphlet is more explicit and exclusive, and, if mastered, makes the Alhambra ever after familiar and easy of comprehension. We carried it about with us as fondly as we had carried Street's book about the cathedrals of Burgos and Toledo.

the same time, religious, warlike, luxurious, sensuous, æsthetic.

If you wish to study Moorish art in detail, take in hand one of the beautiful marqueterie, or *artesonado* ceilings, or a glazed tile, or *azulejo*. In both these cases the history of the word is the history of the thing. *Artesonado* means a kneading-trough; which, doubtless, first suggested the form of these ceilings; and *azulejo* is directly derived from the Arabic word *zuluja*, a varnished tile, and *azul*, which in its turn is derived from *luzmad*, lapis lazuli. Most names for colour in Spanish are derived from the same source in all arts, for as in the case of the *azulejo*, or coloured tile, the teachers of the art had to supply the name. Both *artesonado* roofing and *azulejo* pavements are very Oriental and ancient. We read in the Bible of the houses "cieled with cedar and painted with vermilion," and of the "pavements of saphire," &c.

Nothing can equal the taste and good sense, —always an infallible criterion of art—displayed in both these triumphs of form, colour, and convenience. The tile, which is always of graceful pattern and beautifully enamelled colours, is cool, clean, and exactly the flooring suited for hot climates. Labour both of brain and hand are never spared, for wherever good *azulejo* work exists, there is sure to be plenty of variety, both as to colour and design. But it is chiefly in the *artesonado* ceilings that the Moorish artist is unrivalled. Here his gorgeous fancy runs riot, and the eyes are dazzled by the wonderful combinations of form and colour that have no counterpart save in his equally intricate and equally rich poetry. A verse of the Koran is just as florid and harmonious to the ear of the Arab scholar, as one of their designs must be to the eye of any artist, no matter what his nation may be.

But the simplicity of the original plan is the most striking point to consider. The Arab was as thorough a geometrician as he was an artist, and brought his geometry to bear upon his art in an extraordinary fashion.

Some of the most beautiful tiles and ceilings are to be seen at the Generalife, the summer palace of the kings of Granada. A pretty walk leads to it; and here, even in December, I found the gardens full of roses and other summer flowers in blossom. Granada is indeed a garden of roses; and the Generalife is the lightest, airiest summer-house ever reared by Oriental lover of coolness, and running streams and bosquets of myrtle. It recalls how :—

> " In Xanadu did Kubla Khan
> A stately pleasure-house decree."

But why say more of Granada? After all, descriptions are all but useless. *Vidi tantum!* Having seen the Alhambra, one seems to have seen everything.

CHAPTER X.

PIGS, VULGAR AND ARISTOCRATIC.—THE GIPSY CAPTAIN BEWITCHES US.—WE GO DOWN TO THE POTTER'S HOUSE.—A FAMILY DANCE.—AN AWFUL DISCOVERY.—A BOOKSELLER OF TARSHISH.

I HEARD two horrid stories at Granada, which I would not repeat except that I feel some of their truth. We were walking in the town one day, and observing an unusual air of stir and excitement, asked a stander-by what it meant.

The person in question told us that a certain Señor, Don So-and-so, had just died, and that as he was a great enemy to the Liberal party, and a great tyrant, there was rejoicing among the people. We were interested in the matter, and talked of it afterwards to an old *Granadino*, whose acquaintance we had made during our stay, and he more than confirmed the report.

"He was a bad man," he said, "but of the *sangre azul* (blue blood), a thorough aristocrat, and very powerful. I could tell you stories of what he did that you would not believe. Oh! the people who have blue blood in their veins can do anything in Spain, I assure you. It is a *cosa de España*. Now just listen to a thing this Señor Don L—— did not more than nine years ago. A poor honest man known to me, was taken up accused of committing a theft. He belonged to the Liberal party, and was hated by the blue blood. Well, this man, who is just dead, had him brought into the Plaza de Toos, and tied him up to one of the posts by the hands. 'Did you or did you not commit this theft?' he asked. 'Señor, I know nothing of it. I am as innocent as a child.'" Then this Señor Don —— ordered his man to hammer on to the prisoner's hands with an iron hammer.

"'Did you or did you not commit this theft?' he was asked again by the great gentleman of the blue blood. 'Señor, I have said I am innocent.' Again the hammer fell on the poor man's hands, and again and again, till the bones were broken, and he still denying the deed. At last, finding him so obstinate, they let him go back to prison, where he was kept for weeks. When he came out I saw with my own eyes the ruin they had made of his poor hands."

" But that is as bad as the Inquisition," I said, horrified.

The old man, with a good deal of Spanish punctiliousness, had a touch of Moorish resignation, or what might better be called perhaps fatalism. "We have had to bear such things. I can tell you what happened to me in my youth, when there was still more difference between the law for the blue blood and the white.* I am of the white of course, no Don or Caballero, but a humble Señor, of little account. I was a dealer

* Spain is divided among three populations. First, the aristocracy, or blue blood: as Ford says, satirically, "The azure ichor of this *élite* of the earth is so called in contradistinction to common red blood, the puddle that flows in plebeian veins; while the blood of heretics, Lutherans, Protestants, and political enemies, is held by Spanish sangrados, or heralds, to be black, pitchy, and therefore combustible." A Spaniard gave me the grades thus: blue blood, aristocratic; red blood, middle class; white blood, plebeian.

in pigs, Señoras; and I sold a fine lot of pigs to a certain aristocratic gentleman whom I will call Don Serafin. Don Serafin agreed to buy my pigs for five hundred dollars, paying half the sum down, and giving me a written document engaging to pay the other at the end of three months. My beautiful pigs went, and the three months passed. No money from Don Serafin. As I did not wish to appear impertinent, (being of the white blood, therefore, nobody, you know, Señoras) I waited patiently till three months more had slipped away. Then I waited on Don Serafin, and respectfully demanded my money. 'I owe him money!' cried the great man to his servants, 'turn the impertinent fellow away, *Es un mentira. He lies.*'

"I saw that nothing remained for me but to sue him for my money, which I did. On the day appointed, we appeared before the Alcalde, who received Don Serafin with bows and scrapes, gave him the seat of honour, begged to know to what chance he was indebted for the pleasure of seeing him, and so on. 'Why, it is that fellow there,' said Don Serafin, 'who has brought me here with a cooked-up story about some pigs, *Es un mentira*. I never bought his pigs, or if I did, paid for them long ago. Don't believe a word of it.' The Alcalde then turned to me, who stood by, hat in hand, like a criminal. 'Speak out, *hombre*,' he said, sternly, ' of what do you accuse his grace, Don Serafin de So and so and So and so ' (the blue-blooded race have very long titles, you know). 'Señor,' I said, still standing, ' I sold Don Serafin a lot of beautiful pigs, and he agreed to give five hundred dollars for them, paying half the sum down and the other at the end of three months. Señor, I have never received the last half of the money.' The Alcalde turned to Don Serafin, smiling sweetly ; 'Señor Don Serafin, you hear what this fellow says—is it true or not ?'

"' *Es un mentira*, a pack of lies and nothing more,' again answered his grace Don Serafin ; ' don't believe half a syllable of the story.'

"The Alcalde looked at me with a scowl as if he could devour me.

"' How dare you accuse a gentleman of such a thing ? Get along with you, you lying rogue.'

"I then with great humility brought out the paper signed by Don Serafin himself, in which the money was promised at a certain date. 'Señor,' I said, 'your grace will recognise this writing. The money is a large sum to a poor man like me; I hope you will pay it at once.'

"The Alcalde looked at the paper and was obliged to admit my claim. But he still smiled sweetly on Don Serafin, and looked as fiercely at me as if I were robbing them both.

"Don Serafin tossed back the paper scornfully, and with it a note for fifty dollars. 'You shall have the rest in two months' time,' he said, 'will that satisfy you?'

"'Pardon me, your grace,' I said, 'but I am a poor man and I want the money. It seems, I dare say, but a mere trifle to you, it is a little fortune to me. Please pay me my two hundred and fifty dollars.'

"Don Serafin looked at the Alcalde, making a sign. The Alcalde was silent. 'You fellow, to dictate to me in that way; take the fifty dollars and be thankful to the Virgin; or leave them if you please, I don't care.'

"I turned to the Alcalde and humbly asked his intercession; but it was quite clear I had little enough to expect of him. He seemed to think I was mighty lucky to get anything at all; so, after standing in the presence of the great man till I was ready to drop, I took the fifty dollars and went away."

"And did you ever get the remaining two hundred dollars?" I asked.

He shook his head.

"No, Signorita, not I. I got a part, ten dollars one month, ten another, and so on, but never the whole. *Es una cosa de España.* We of the white blood must submit to those of the blue."

These stories are both worth something as testimony of things as they are, or very lately were, in Spain, and we heard others which I remember less clearly.

There are a great many gipsies at Granada still, and, though they have lost their prestige for romance and daring, a good deal of interest is attached to them. They seem now to be held as very inoffensive sort of people, are miserably

o

poor, dirty, and live troglodyte fashion, in caves hollowed in the hill-side. The King of the Gipsies, or *El Capitan* as he is called, is a fine musician, and we invited him to come up to the hotel one evening and play to us. Captain Antonio's company is not to be had for the asking. He is, or affects to be, a little shy, wants coaxing and persuading, will not play except before a large audience; and, as Bensaken said to us, "He is a great man in his way, and you couldn't offer him less than two dollars."

After disappointing us on several occasions, Captain Antonio came. He had pleaded a sore finger as excuse for his delay, but I am inclined to think that he waited in expectation of a larger audience and more dollars; for the arrival of an American family healed the Captain's finger miraculously fast. It was sore in the morning, very bad indeed! and, lo and behold! in the evening it was quite well; but let that pass—Captain Antonio's music made us very forgiving.

He came in—a tall, superbly built man in the prime of life, with a tawny skin, eyes of extraordinary brilliancy, receding jaws, and very low brow, long narrow throat, and altogether, of an Egyptian, ancient look, as if he had been one of the old Nile gods come to life.

He bowed graciously, threw off his Spanish cloak, for the gitanos, like all the rest of the world, are growing conventional now, losing costume and characteristics every day ; and commenced tuning his guitar.

It was a wretchedly poor instrument, and we began to wonder what sort of torments were about to be inflicted on us, when, on a sudden, the tuning ceased and the music seized hold of us like galvanism. For it was such music as one had never dreamed of before. His fingers but touch the chords, and all at once your breath is taken away, your blood is warmed as if by strong wine, your brain whirls, your eyes see visions, your ears hear marvellous voices, your senses are all mastered by a power that seems to shake the very spheres.

You see the strangest forms and faces, imp, devil, witch, and wizard ; you hear a jargon of voices, in love, in anger, in war, in worship, in joy, in despair. Beautiful gitanos come in the charmed circle, join hands, dance for a moment and vanish, or it is filled by a gipsy camp—the fires are blazing, you see men and women feasting, singing, making love, when, all at once, a cry of alarm is heard, and the scene is changed to bloodshed and horrors. Every phase of savage life is brought before your eyes and made real, as if you were tasting it in the flesh. You are indeed for the nonce a gipsy, and know what the gipsy's world is, above, below, in heaven and in hell; your pulses are quickened to gipsy pitch, you are ready to make love and war, to heal and slay, to wander to the world's end, to be outlawed and hunted down, to dare and do anything for the sake of the sweet, untrammelled life of the tent, the bright blue sky, the mountain air, the free savagedom, the joyous dance, the passionate friendship, the fiery love.

All at once the gipsy stopped, and the spell was broken. We had never been gipsies, after all; the camp-fires burning under the dark night, the flashing knives, the peaceful dance, the happy loves, the vagabond wanderings over plain and mountain, the midnight encounter,—all these had been but shadows evoked by Captain Antonio's guitar, and we were a company of ladies and gentlemen, whose utmost vagabondage had not exceeded boiling a pic-nic kettle in Epsom Forest, or, more likely, taking tea on our own lawns. We felt thankful to Señor Antonio for having given us so full an experience of wild life in the space of a few minutes. I cannot say how real it had all seemed. We had wandered with him over so many southern lands, had bivouacked under such fiery suns, that I looked at a fair-haired English lady present, almost with a feeling of wonder to see her hair still golden and her cheeks still rosy.

The gipsy captain received our expressed thanks, as I thought, indifferently, but looked into our faces as if he would read our real criticisms there. Whether he approved either of them or of us, it were quite impossible to say; he had a face as unreadable as a bit of hieroglyphic writing, except that whilst playing, a strange fiery light shone in his eyes, as if he were himself possessed by the devilry of his music.

When he had rested a little and drunk a *copita*, or thimbleful of brandy, we asked him for a sacred song, and he said he would play us a Christmas hymn. What a change! It was as touching and sweet a melody as any of our Christmas carols, and quite as solemn.

By-and-by some one proposed a dance. Would Captain Antonio oblige us by a bolero or fandango? Most readily, he answered, but he must have a partner; of course,—so we went down into the kitchen, and, after much pressing, up came the daughters of the house, Pepita and little Pepita, Maria, and a friend as young and pretty and playful as themselves. The brother, our little waiter, threw aside his napkin and took up the gipsy's guitar as naturally as if he had been a musician by profession; one of the young ladies, after a little coyness, consented to become Captain Antonio's partner, and the dance commenced,—that musical, monotonous dance, so popular among the pleasure-loving Andalusians. But to gain a thorough idea of a gipsy dance, you must get up what is called a *funcion*,—rather a costly affair; that is to say, you must invite a troop of gipsies, who will not come to dance and sing and play to you without being well paid. Captain Antonio every one should hear and see; he is quite a genius, and if enticed to London or Paris, would create a sensation. We said to him,—

"You should purchase a better guitar, Señor Antonio, and go to London. You would come home a rich man."

He smiled, showing his glittering white teeth and shook his head :—

"I have a wife and five children, Señora," he replied ; " London is too far off."

And he did not like the disparagement of his guitar, I think, for he took it up and tuned it in a caressing sort of way, as if it were a living pet we had been slighting.

There is nothing of romance left to the gipsies in Spain now but their costume, even that fast disappearing, and their music. When Borrow wrote of them more than sixty years ago, he speaks of the happy effects of Charles the Third's edicts, which, by admitting the gipsies into the pale of civilised society, has done more than the fierce persecutions of his predecessors to assimilate this savage race with others. Ferdinand and Isabella and the Philips, did their utmost to put down what they called the Egyptians, publishing edict after edict against them, but in vain. Whilst they were a proscribed caste, whilst the very privilege of sanctuary was denied them, whilst they were hunted down and persecuted by fire and sword, the Egyptians, or Gitanos, flourished and had their palmy days; murdering, stealing, cheating, telling fortunes, hating the Busnees, and all who were not Romanys, to their heart's content. *Gitanisimo*—that is to say, quoting Borrow, gipsy villany of every description, flourished till *Gitanisimo* was declared to be no more. Charles the Third, in 1733, published a humane edict in which he declared the gipsies capable of following any career of arts and sciences, and altogether ignored that they were a separate people, amenable to separate laws. What was the consequence? *The law of Carlos Tercero has superseded gipsy law*, say the gipsies a little regretfully. *Gitanisimo*, or gipsydom, if not wholly transformed, has been modified. The gipsies no longer wander about living by murder and theft. The women still tell fortunes, and the men, as dealers in horses and mules, are not to be trusted, but they are everywhere spoken of as a poor and harmless set of people; and though the instinct of caste is just as strong as ever among themselves, they are no longer feared or hated. At the time Borrow wrote the gipsies in Spain numbered 40,000 souls; at the commencement of the present century they numbered only 20,000, so that the race here, as elsewhere, seems dying out, or, at any rate, greatly decreasing. Indeed, nothing else could have been expected of them. Wild animals from African deserts are not more out of place, caged in English gardens, than these kings and queens of savagedom compelled to sleep under a roof, and to consider killing as murder. But their dancing and music are worthy of a less lawless and terrible race, and are *cosas de España,* not to be missed by any travellers.

In the afternoon we drove to the Albaycin, or old town, in search of pottery. The views from this part of Granada are very fine, but the inhabitants are so unused to the sight of travellers, and are such strange, half-civilised beings, that you are hardly able to see anything. We alighted in one place to walk a few yards, and in a moment, as wasps gather round a fallen peach, we were surrounded by a youthful rabble who looked at us suspiciously, and not content with that, caught hold of our clothes, begged from us, laughed at us—all but tore us to pieces. We had left our coachman behind, as we had come by a way not *carrossable,* in order to see a view, and our poor old guide was wholly inefficient to keep off the tribe of persecutors. Two or three big gipsyish girls of twelve or thirteen, caught hold of his coat, and I expected to see his pockets attacked every moment. The noise and noisomeness of this dirty, unkempt mob of juveniles no words can describe. Bensaken's mild reproof, " Are not these señoras like other señoras ? why do you behave so rudely to them ?" had no effect. We lost temper, shook our umbrellas threateningly, scolded, and pushed on, never waiting to see the view, and only too glad to close the carriage-door on the merciless, miserable little rabble. Any Englishwoman venturing alone in the streets of the Albaycin would have reason to regret such a piece of audacity as long as she lived. I believe she would be pelted with mud and stones. Nothing is too bad to expect from those awful children. What are the priests after, that they are left in such a state of savage-dom?

But the Albaycin has pleasanter aspects. Bensaken now took us to a little spot far away from the scene of our persecution, and we soon found ourselves in a scene so peaceful, so poetic, and so lovely, that the ugly dream faded away from our memories. It was the potter's house we had come to see. The outer walls were white-washed and bare, after the fashion of Moorish houses, but no sooner was the threshold passed than all was life and colour.

Picture to yourselves a sunny little court with a fountain in the midst, pots of flowers here and there, dogs basking in the sun, pigeons fluttering over head, and rows of lustrous pottery, blue, green, yellow, and brown, placed against the walls, or heaped up in the corners. We entered a little sitting-room and were made welcome by the whole family. There was a grandmother, an aunt, a cousin, and I do not know how many more, but I am only concerned with the young potter and his mother. The first was a lad of nineteen, with quite an artist's face, sensitive, refined, full of happy expression; the second was a handsome, portly creature, a regular type of the Andalusian matron, and as ready to sing or dance a bolero, as the youngest of her daughters.

We were enchanted with the pottery, which is often rude in shape and colouring, but never without a certain childish grace and feeling for art. Some of the designs are wonderfully good, bold, simple, and unique, whilst the coloured patterns often testify a richness of fancy and comprehension of decorative art, quite astonishing in artists so untaught. The prevailing colour is dark rich blue, reminding one of old Wedgwood, and there is always a liberality of imagination both in shape and ornament; no vases or dishes are alike either in the one respect or the other. But, alas! cheap as this quaint pottery is, and plentiful as it would be if appreciated, the manufactures of France and England are taking its place, and by-and-by travellers will have to look far and wide for specimens of it.

The boy seemed delighted at our appreciation of his work, and took us into his atelier. It reminded us of the prophet who said, "I went down into the potter's house, and he wrought a work on the wheels," the place was so primitive and Eastern. The young potter sat down at his work, and fashioned a dish for us ; then he took up one already "tried in the fire," and showed us his manner of colouring. It was quite beautiful to see the dexterity with which he worked, and the fondness with which he regarded his work. We tried our hand and found the matter not so easy as it had appeared.

When we had seen enough and made our purchases, noticing a guitar that lay near, we asked for some music. The request was granted smilingly. Our young potter sat down and played a fandango, his mother and one of the younger women dancing for us. They were all so kindly pleasant, and so amused at being able to amuse us.

We bade these nice people adieu with some regret, and hoped that all other travellers would be guided by some lucky star to their pretty Moorish "potter's house." It was pretty enough to make us forget all other diabolical spirits haunting the Albaycin, or old town of Granada.

In the modern town, there is little to be

seen excepting a very beautiful old Moorish *passage*, with horse-shoe arches, sculptured friezes, and delicate marble columns. Of course, this will soon be a thing of tradition only, but whilst it lasts, it is perfectly Eastern and very picturesque. I went out shopping several times, though it requires an effort to quit the fairy-like region of the Alhambra, and descend into such dingy, ill-paved, smelling streets.

One morning, to our infinite consternation, we found that we had come to an end of our books. We looked into each other's faces with dismay, and turned over our treasures again and again. Yes, it was but too true. We had read Ford from beginning to end, we had read *Don Quixote*, we had read our beloved Street, our Stirling, our Borrow, our one volume of Wordsworth, our guides and geographies, our *Vie de Cervantes*, again and again; and last, but not least, our Benjamin of books, viz., Owen Jones' *Handbook to the Alhambra*. We had even devoured with avidity some odd chapters of French novels, given for translation into Spanish, in a little book recommended to me by my Spanish master in Madrid. And as to newspapers, a number of the *Petit Journal* would have been a mine of wealth to us, in this intellectual desert. We had purchased a stray copy of a Granada paper, grandiosely called, *El Triumfo Granadino*, and found it a very poor affair indeed, made up of gossip, poor jokes, advertisements, and feuilleton.

We were confidently assured that there were books in plenty to be obtained in the town, English, French, or in Spanish, so I set off in the search, Bensaken accompanying me.

"Mind," said my friend, "and bring home something light, witty, and entertaining. A good French novel or two, or one of the last Tauchnitz editions."

I promised to do my best, but experience proved that there was no judgment to be exercised in the matter. It was simply a case of Hobson's choice. There was only one bookseller's shop, and in that bookseller's shop was only one book—that is to say, available book. The bookseller, a very nonchalant person indeed, smoked a cigarette, and chatted with a neighbour, whilst I investigated his stock in trade.

On the first shelf stood a row of school-books and penny parts of cheap illustrated editions of Cervantes, Paul de Koch, Eugene Sue, and *Gil Blas*; on the second, were a few novels of Alex. Dumas, fils, in the well-known green covers, at a franc each; on the third, were, firstly, Victor Hugo's *Travailleurs de Mer*; secondly, an odd volume of Byron; thirdly, the American edition of Washington Irving's *Tales of the Alhambra*; fourthly, an English story, called *Once and Again*, published by Tauchnitz. The first-named books we had, of course, read; but oh! how greedily I seized upon that little English story, and carried it home with me! How we gloried in the possession of it, and glowed over the love-story of it! The book was by no means stirring as a story, or first-rate as a work of art, but we had been living without novels for months past, and it was like being made quite youthful again. If ever it be my fate to meet the author of that little story in the flesh, I mean to thank her for the pleasure she gave us in a bookless "city of Tarshish."

CHAPTER XI.

THE ARCHBISHOP BLESSES THE ENGINE, AND WE HELP HIM. — DELIGHTFUL LOJA. — A FUNNY DINNER. — STARLIGHT, TWILIGHT, MORNING.

WE "had heard, but not believed," that the line of railway between Granada and Malaga, as far as Loja, was to be opened on or about the day we proposed leaving; and we determined that, if the train really ran, we would be among its first passengers. But oh! the dreary difficulty of learning anything from anybody about anything in Spain! We ran hither and thither, we despatched messenger after messenger, but in vain; "*No sé*," I know nothing — was the invariable answer received in each case, and the nearer the time approached, the greater seemed the uncertainty. But had it not been officially announced, and were we not bound to believe an official announcement in official Spain, however at fault individual information might be? So we

P

quietly allowed all doubts and disbeliefs to clear from our minds, and declared our intention of proceeding to Loja by the first train, trusting to miracles that the train would run. There is nothing like trusting to miracles in Spain. You are promised that such and such a thing shall be done; you speculate anxiously, it may be, but of necessity, curiously, as to the how and the when; you wait, and wait, and wait, and without any apparent intervention, the thing grows up like the prophet's gourd.

So it was in this case. Nobody took any trouble about the train; no one seemed responsible for the starting of the train; no one but ourselves wanted to start by the train, and yet, after all, the train went. It was like the old nursery story—water wouldn't quench fire, fire wouldn't burn stick, stick wouldn't beat pig, pig wouldn't get over the stile, and on a sudden water began to quench fire, fire began to burn stick, stick began to beat pig, etc.

The train was to start for Loja at twelve o'clock precisely, but, of course, we were driven to the station a good hour and a half in advance. What a laughable scene it was! All the wags of Granada had come out to see the train start, quite believing, I am sure, that it would not start that day. The Andalusian is light-hearted, ready-witted, and prone to say smart things. Here was a fine occasion of quibs and puns, and it was not neglected. The train was treated like a charlatan or tumbler who has promised to perform a certain trick, and at the eleventh hour would fain call off. Every one and every thing connected with it came in for a share of raillery, the priests who were to consecrate it, the guards who were to drive it, the stokers who were to keep it going, the passengers who were going by it, and the crowd who came to see it.

The very beasts of burden seemed to be in league against that unfortunate train. We had driven down to the station in an omnibus drawn by two handsome mules, that had been docile as possible on former occasions, but, like all true-born Granadinos, they were thorough-going conservatives, and would have nothing whatever to say to the train. So, no sooner had we got in sight of the engine and line of carriages, than they kicked, pranced, and, finally, ran right into a ditch. They were stormed at, whipped, pulled, and coaxed out somehow; but neither blows nor entreaties could induce them to move a step nearer the platform. This incident naturally offered food for merriment to the wags, who seemed divided between their admiration of the mules who wouldn't approach the train, and of amusement at the unfortunate travellers whom they had upset. Having, after some delay, procured our tickets, we crossed over to the platform, where a little crowd was already assembled to witness the inaugural ceremony. By-and-by, two or three sacristans appeared and erected a temporary altar, trimming it with gay artificial flowers and ribbon. Then there was a pause of some minutes, at the end of which came the Archbishop of Granada, dressed in gorgeous purple vestments, accompanied by several priests. The Archbishop had a grand look, irrespective of his robes. He was an old man with beautiful features and a pure, intellectual expression. The priests would have looked coarse and commonplace anywhere, but by the side of him they looked doubly so; indeed a stronger term than either of these might have been applied to them.

They had almost a vicious look. And now the candles were lighted, the Archbishop put on his mitre, the crowd fell on their knees and the ceremony began. A litany was chanted first of all, I think; then a prayer was read; and, last of all, the engine was sprinkled with holy water, and the crowd received a benediction. Everybody seemed a little *distrait* except the good old Archbishop, which was, perhaps, natural. How could people think of anything serious at such an exciting time?

As soon as the consecration had finished the train really did start, and great was the stir and loud the cheering, as we began to move off. It was a sight to see the wall of eager faces on either side of us as we glided slowly out of Granada. There were old men and women of ninety, who held up their trembling hands and called on the Virgin in wonder; there were *gamins* and children of all sizes, who stood open-mouthed at the sight; there were middle-aged peasants from the mountains, who became children, too, in their great bewilderment. If only a John Leech had been there to see and to sketch!

The cheers and shouts broke out intermittingly all the way to Loja, like the signal fires that told of the taking of Troy from Asia to Greece. At every village or station, or convenient point of sight, had collected crowds of peasants, ladies in mantillas, priests, *arrieros*, and all seemed disposed to welcome the new era.

The journey to Loja was beautiful. We had a good view of the Sierra Nevada for the greater part of the way, and the fields of snow lying lightly on the lapis lazuli mountains had a dreamy and sweet effect.

We reached Loja in about two hours. All the town had turned out to see the train come in, and the platform was a gay scene with its tiers of brightly-dressed ladies, fanning themselves in the sun. Spanish crowds are never in a hurry to disperse, so we quietly waited half-an-hour in our cosy carriage, by the end of which time we saw a little room on the platform for ourselves, our bags, and our books.

A good-tempered, well-dressed man packed the latter on his donkey's back, and accompanied us to the town, about three-quarters of a mile from the station. It was a very pretty walk along the river-side, and the sky was of brilliant burning blue. Our light water-proof travelling cloaks were much too warm.

Loja is very interesting and beautiful. We should like to have remained there a month. The Parador was not a luxurious place; but if white-washed walls, brick floors nicely sanded, a wash-hand basin, and clean beds, are not enough to satisfy a weary traveller, what would be? We rested on our beds delightfully for an hour, and then descended to see if there was any possibility of getting mules and saddles for a little excursion. But there was none: so, taking a guide with us, we set out on foot. We strolled first through the narrow, crooked, Moorish-like streets to the river-side, where we found a scene quite unique in tone and colour. From the side of a lofty rock issued ten springs of crystal water, and around each were gathered peasant women, in red and yellow petticoats, busily washing their gay rags of clothing in the sunset. The brilliant hues of the sky, the gay dresses of the women, the dark rocks, the limpid river, the old Moorish fort that towered above all, made a picture not easily to be forgotten; but when we had climbed to the fort, and looked across the Alpuxarras flaming in the last rays of the sun, and the bright green plain below, and the river narrowing to a thread in the distance, we thought we had seen no more beautiful view in Spain. The fort is now turned into a prison, and to reach the rampart we had to pass through a low, gloomy room, full of soldiers and convicts returning from their day's labour on the railway. Wherever there is road-making or rail-making to be done in Spain, you see lines of prisoners at work linked in twos and fours, under strong military surveillance; which seems a healthy and profitable prison system. We sat down on a broken wall overgrown with prickly cactus, and watched the sun set over mountain and plain, river and village, whilst our guide chatted with the soldiers about themselves, their neighbours, and their doings. A Spanish guide is not in the least conventional. He undertakes to conduct you to a certain place, and there his responsibility ends; he does not bore you with historical and geographical facts; he never knows anything about anything; he picks up a companion on the way, and, whilst smoking his tiny cigarette, talks over the affairs of the place. Our present cicerone was no exception to this rule. He had called for a friend as we came through the town, and the two young men, who were very intelligent and well-mannered, seemed to enjoy the walk as much as we did. They spoke no French, of course; but our imperfect Spanish never elicited a smile from them. The Moro-Andalusian has certainly imbibed dignity of bearing as well as other good things from the Arab.

After enjoying to the utmost the magical splendours of the sunset and the sweet mountain air that seemed to blow from all corners of the earth, we descended to the town and our parador. We were somewhat footsore, and no wonder; for the pavement of Loja is a sort of hardbake, of flints and stone.

At six o'clock we descended to dinner, and what a funny dinner it was! The *comedor*, or *salle à manger*, was as big as a barn, and at the upper end sat ten commercial travellers, laughing and talking with the black-eyed, noisy mistress of the house. The cloth had been laid just anyhow, and the dishes were brought on anyhow too. We helped ourselves to plates and knives, and then to whatever came in the way. The fare was certainly bountiful. First, came soup; secondly, the favourite dish of *lengua de vaca*, or hot ox-tongue; thirdly, an odd mess of cabbage and broth; fourthly, pork—for the Spaniards, as Ford says, combine Bacon with Belief,—not good; fifthly, partridges, very good; lastly, raisins, figs, cakes, and coffee. But it was the behaviour of our landlady that made the dinner so entertaining. She seemed to think it incumbent upon her, being hostess, to keep her guests in a roar of laughter, *ab ovo usque ad mala*. She spoke so fast, and used so many proverbs, and provincial expressions, that it was very difficult to catch her meaning; but she went over the ground again for our benefit sometimes, and seemed delighted to make us laugh too. Proverb followed proverb, repartee came after repartee, story after story, till the peals of laughter became so deafening that we were glad to retire to our rooms.

Will it be believed that we had to wait till midnight for the diligence? Fancy having to wait at Tavistock ten hours for the Launceston coach! But the truth is, that the railway company and the diligence company don't like each other at all, and between them both unfortunate travellers have a hard time of it. We had to pay the full diligence fare from Granada to Malaga, though we only took places from Loja to Malaga, and the railway fare for the two hours journey from Granada to Loja was so high that I verily believe we paid the whole railway fare too. I name this imposition as an exceptional fact in our Spanish experiences. We had both travelled a good deal, in America, Algeria, Italy, Germany, and we were constantly saying to ourselves, when discussing the matters of bills, waiters, porterage, and all other things incidental to travellers, "They manage these things better in Spain." I cannot too strongly condemn the unfair assertions of English travellers about Spain and the Spaniards; and I name the Grenada-Loja-Malaga Unlimited Travellers' Discomfort Company, because the treatment we received at their hands was wholly unprecedented throughout our travels in the Peninsula.

But the waiting at Loja was by no means disagreeable, even when night came on, for we lay on our comfortable beds, and drowsed and dreamed till midnight, when we were suddenly aroused by the diligence dashing up the street, horn blowing, bells jingling, whips cracking, driver hallooing. The noise was so sudden, and so infernal, that the very night seemed too disturbed to settle into silence again. To add to it, in rushed our hostess hurried and excited to such a pitch that you would have fancied it must be at least an earthquake that so disturbed her, crying, "La diligencia! La diligencia!" "Yes," we said, quietly putting on our bonnets, "we heard it."

But she did not heed our answer, and rushed about the room, snatching up our bags and bundles, knocking down coffee-cups and glasses, and still crying "La diligencia! La diligencia!" The broken crockery and the spilt coffee only increased her agitation, and she dashed out of the room as she had dashed in, leaving us no little amused and amazed at so much energy displayed upon so trifling an occasion.

We quite enjoyed the journey to Malaga. First

Dawn. 221

came the starlight and the weird, wild aspect of plain and sierra; then the cold grey dawn and the re-creation of the world from end to end; then the lovely flush of sunrise over the many-coloured hills, as if of altar fires raised to the Power that had created them.

CHAPTER XII.

WE GET TO ALGECIRAS, AND ARE MADE WRETCHED.—THE FAT SPANIARD AND THE LEAN ENGLISHMAN.—A RED-LETTER DAY AT GIBRALTAR.—THE LIGHTS.—ADIEU TO EUROPE.

ALL the old difficulties about boats recommenced at Malaga; and, much as we disliked the place, which seemed to have grown dustier and fishier since we had left it, we were obliged to remain there several days. At last we learned somehow that there was a boat, named the *Adriana*, doing weekly services between Malaga and Algeciras, and Malaga and Tangiers, and that, as all communication by sea between Malaga and Gibraltar had ceased on account of the cholera, on the *Adriana* we must build all our hopes.

But, as luck would have it, she had left the harbour just as we had come in, so that there was nothing to do but await her return, and pray for fair weather. What made our very fates, as it were, hang upon the *Adriana*, was the information received by telegram that a boat left Gibraltar for Oran on the following Friday. It was now Monday, and, according to all accounts, the *Adriana* was to return on Tuesday or Wednesday, and go to Algeciras the next day. But Tuesday passed, and Wednesday came; and people prophesied bad weather; and the *Adriana* did not appear. Cervantes and his fellow-captives at Algiers hardly looked oftener for the ship that was to deliver them, than did we for the *Adriana*. We were always running down to the beach and straining our eyes after some imaginary sail. But none appeared; and we were dining in rather a melancholy state at the prospect of losing our boat to Oran, when the master of the hotel sent us a message that the *Adriana* had arrived, and would set out for Algeciras at seven o'clock next morning.

We had splendid weather for the trip. The dawn was grey and pearly, and from its heart, like some gorgeous bird slowly soaring from a dusky nest, arose the warm, brilliant, southern day. The sea was smooth as a lake; the sky of deepest, warmest blue; the mountains, of loveliest form and colour; the little sailing boats, fairy things, seen in so enchanted a scene and atmosphere! Words, indeed, fail to give any idea of this beautiful coast scenery; but it must be seen on such a day as we saw it.

One is not accustomed to think much of the beauty of Gibraltar, and the first sight of it was quite a surprise to me. The Cornish coast has no finer view than this colossal mass of limestone rock, and the colour of it, so grey and silvery, and so soft, against a light-blue sky, is something indescribable.

We had been assured again and again that we should reach Algeciras in time to get into Gibraltar that night; but, as the afternoon wore on, public opinion on board veered. The captain, who seemed quite confident about the matter at noon, shook his head gravely an hour later.

"You doubt," I said, "whether we shall reach Algeciras in time, or whether we shall find means of getting into Gibraltar?"

"I doubt both," he replied.

"But," I continued, "we are going to start for Oran by the steamer that leaves Gibraltar to-morrow. It is absolutely necessary that we get into Gibraltar to-night, or the steamer may have left."

"I don't say that you can't do it, Señora," he said; "but there are difficulties. It is difficult to get into Gibraltar by sea at all, on account of the quarantine, and after four o'clock it is impossible." He pulled out his watch. "I am afraid by the time we reach Algeciras it will be too late for that. As to riding round the bay, if we get into harbour in pretty good time, and if you can get horses, and if it is tolerably light, why you can do it, of course."

There was nothing to do but wait; but the Captain's prognostics proved true. We did not reach Algeciras in time to get into Gibraltar—supposing there had been boats to take us, which there were not; and as to the latter part of his speech, that was also true; for there was no obstacle in the way of riding round the bay that night, except that there were no horses; and if there had been horses, there was no time; and if there had been time, there was no light.

There is only one inn at Algeciras, and hither flocked all the unhappy passengers by the *Adriana*, clamouring for horses, mules, boats, guides, anything so long as they could get into Gibraltar that night.

It was a cry of "A horse, a horse, a kingdom for a horse!" you would have fancied that everybody's life hung upon getting into Gibraltar. I think some gentlemen did get horses, but they were exceptions; and the little inn was so crowded as to present the appearance of a camp. Beds were made up *ex improviso* all over the house, and we had to content ourselves with a hole of a room, boasting neither window nor chimney, nor chair, nor table, nor, indeed, any furniture but two beds, and fleas innumerable.

Before retiring to this cell for the night, however, we had a very good dinner, seasoned with some racy gossip of Gibraltar life. We were too tired to dine at the *table d'hôte* (if you are wise, avoid *table d'hôtes* when possible), and preferred to eat the crumbs that fell from other travellers' tables afterwards. These were served to us in a pleasant little *comedor*, looking towards beautiful, inhospitable Gibraltar, with its thousand lights shining like tiers of stars above the dark blue bay. The waiter, who called himself an Englishman, though on what grounds I cannot precisely determine—perhaps because he was born in sound of Gibraltar gun-fire—served the dinner, and then sat down to see us eat. He was so young, so evidently overworked, and so unconventional as a waiter, that we took this familiarity as a matter of course, and listened to what he had to say.

"You seem to be the only waiter in the place," we said; "how do you manage to attend upon everybody?"

He sighed a very long sigh.

"Yes, it's awful work," he said, in his queer Gibraltar English, "since the Quarantine regulation keeps everybody out of Gib. I am ready to drop of fatigue now, and this has been going on for weeks. We don't get to bed till midnight, and we are up at four or five o'clock in the morning, and sleep just anywhere. The Quarantine is worse than the cholera, ten times."

"You are English?" I asked, a little cautiously.

"The Lord be praised, I am! Oh! the Spaniards are a bad set, I assure you; and don't we pitch into 'em when we get a chance! It was not very long ago that we had a regular fight, six Englishmen against six Spaniards, all of us young men, and the Spaniards came off very shabbily. We killed one outright."

"How shocking! but do you mean to say that the police don't interfere?"

"That's as it happens. The English have no business here in Algeciras, you know, and if the Spanish gendarmes disturbed themselves whenever knives are drawn, they'd have an uneasy time of it."

He went on to tell us some more stories about the state of society in Algeciras, which we took *cum grano salis*, having no personal experience of it.

"Shall I not take mine ease at mine inn?" was not applicable to the unfortunate people whom unhospitable Gib. had driven into Algeciras. We dined pretty well because we were not dainty; but so stringent were the Quarantine regulations, that such refreshing luxuries as lemonade, vegetables, and fresh fruits could not be had for love or money. Whatever we asked for, and we only asked for very simple things, "was at Gibraltar;" indeed, everything was at Gibraltar—except the fleas.

We went to bed early, having ordered horses and Spanish saddles at six o'clock next morning; but the fleas would let us have no sleep. There was no armour against them but Spanish patience. Glad indeed were we when morning came, and, after a hasty toilet and a cup of horrible coffee, we descended to the street, being informed that the horses were ready. The word *ready* does not however bear its English signification in Spain. If you have ordered a horse in England and you are told it is ready, you know that you have only to put on hat and gloves and mount. In Spain, it suffices for an animal to exist, or for a thing to be known to be somewhere, and they are both ready. We had made, perhaps, an unwise bargain, but the only one that seemed possible to make, in ordering horses of two proprietors, two of a very big Spaniard and one of a very small Englishman. Of course this led to all sorts of complications, but I must tell my story from the beginning. In the first place, on being told that the horses were ready, and not finding them on the spot, we sent a man to look after the lad who had gone to look after the little boy who had gone to look after the horses that the Spaniard and Englishman had promised to send, but didn't. When the man had come back to say that the lad told him that the little boy told him that the men told him they were coming, we resigned ourselves for a little while, and, by-and-by, the men and the horses did indeed come. But then ensued an altercation as fierce as any detailed by Homer. It was like the fable of the big boy with the little coat, and the little boy with the big coat. The Englishman's horse was small, but he had only a large saddle, and the Spaniard had only a small saddle for a very large horse. There was what is popularly called a "row," and the inhabitants of Algeciras turned out like a swarm of bees to see and hear and take part in it. This commotion lasted nearly an hour, and not till two hours from the time of our descent into the street did we set off.

The ride round the bay was so full of gracious, soothing beauty, that we soon forgot all the discomforts gone through before. The atmosphere of early morning is always delicious in the South; and, to-day, the pale blue bay, the green heights, the glistening white sands, the terraced city, and the grey rocks, seen through so transparent a medium, looked more like a reflexion of a beautiful scene than a scene itself.

We rode quite close to the water's edge, and the musical plashing of the waves, and the sweetness and softness of the air, would have healed any weariness of flesh and spirit, I think. We were weary enough at starting, but had grown quite fresh and strong by the time we had reached the " Lines."

The only drawback to this delightful ride was the garrulousness of my guide. The fat Spaniard had placed himself, with all the baggage, on his strongest horse, and led the way, looking the picture of slothful, self-indulgent *nonchalance*; my friend rode his second horse, comfortably mounted on a Spanish saddle; I followed on the little Englishman's horse, a small, incapable beast, who had evidently been over-worked and ill-fed during the last few busy weeks.

There are some people, luckily very few, who inspire one with instinctive repugnance, and this little Englishman, as he called himself, was one. He was so small, freckled, and ugly, so conceited, and so envious of the big Spaniard, that he reminded one of the frog in Æsop's fables, which tried to blow itself out to the size of the ox.

"Look at that fellow going there," he said in his queer Gibraltar English, and pointing to his enemy; "he is the worst man in the world, and would as soon stick a knife into you as look at you. Just because I set up as horse-dealer and letter, he spites me so that he would kill me if he dared; but I'm an Englishman, and he just knows that he'd better keep his hands off me. He is as mad as a hornet because you English ladies employed me, although he hadn't another horse in the world. When English travellers come to Algeciras, whom do you suppose they would employ, Señora, an Englishman or a Spaniard?"

"Why, I suppose they would pick the best

horses," I replied wickedly; "that is the most important point."

He looked at his own poor brute a little ruefully. "I'd back my horse against any in Gibraltar when he is fresh," he said, "but he went this same journey late last night, and has been hacking at it for days."

"Precisely," I answered, "he can only just put one foot before the other, and if the saddle hurts him as much as it does me, the sooner I get off the better for both of us."

"Yes, I know the saddle goes badly," he went on in the same aggrieved tone; "but it's all that bad man's fault. His saddle just fits Bobby here, and this one is just twice too big. I ran home and got the very pillows from under my wife's head, who is ill of ague, but they slip off like nothing."

"I'm sorry you robbed your wife of her pillows," I said; "but, pillows or no pillows, my saddle is as uneven as a gridiron, whilst the Señora yonder rides as comfortably as possible."

"Oh! yes; that bad man is rich, you know, and can afford to have everything nice. It's just such men as he who eat up poor young beginners like us."

"Of course," I answered, coolly; "the man may be bad or good, but so long as he supplies good horses and comfortable saddles, he'll find customers —though he is a Spaniard, and were to run a knife into somebody every night." And with this conclusion, we concluded.

We were now on English ground, and fancied ourselves in England. The change happened all on a sudden. We had been in Spain a few minutes back. Spain was not a hundred yards off, and now we were at home, among home-like faces, friendly voices, and familiar scenes; and over our heads, on the crest of the grand old rock waved the jolly "Union Jack." There was a hunt outside the town, and we met parties of officers in scarlet, accompanied by fair-haired girls, managing their thoroughbreds as only Englishwomen can; groups of red-haired, clear-complexioned Highlanders, stood about the camps, and the infantine population of some English village seemed out at play on the grass; sturdy housewives were cooking, washing, and nursing babies in the tents; the roads were no longer break-neck bridle-tracks, but real, broad, smooth roads, hard and fit for use; the Spanish soldier, in tight mocassins and short brown cloak, had disappeared as if by magic, giving way to the scarlet coat and the tartan.

The "Spanish lines" are, indeed, no more nor less than a handful of houses called by courtesy the town of La Linea. In Ford's time, La Linea consisted of " a few miserable hovels, the lair of greedy officials, who live on the crumbs of Gibraltar ;" at least so he writes of it in 1839, but we were assured that there is a decent inn at La Linea now, and that it is quite possible for belated travellers to sleep there. The contrast between Spain and England—two opposed countries placed in such strange juxtaposition—is most striking. You pass in five minutes from a land of sleepy, blissful lethargy to a stirring, bustling, look-alive sea-port and garrison town. I dare say Gibraltar would not be a pleasant place to live in, but after spending so many weeks among people who think nothing in the world worth hurrying about, and no one's time of the slightest importance whatever, it was delightful to breathe the business-like, martial air of the place. You cannot help doing in Spain as the Spaniards do, and by the time you have traversed the length and breadth of Old Castile and Andalusia, you must be of a very unimpressionable temperament indeed if you have not imbibed the *genius loci*,.that indescribable Oriental habit of living from morning to night without the least inclination to trouble oneself about anything under the sun.

Here, in Gibraltar, you feel at once subjected to the military spirit that rules it. The streets are alive with music; the sharp fife, the warlike cornet, the rolling drum; there is always a "recall" being sounded, or a *réveillé*, or a gun being fired. You might fancy war was going on from the constant bustling to and fro of regiments and recurrence of signals. And there is a stirring air about the streets which is quite new. The town is alive with people, all intent on business or pleasure, and if you have any business on hand, you find means of doing it quickly and satisfactorily.

The day was delicious, and at the Club-house Hotel we were met by my friend's cousin, Colonel ———, who carried us off to his pretty house outside the town, and introduced us to his wife and beautiful little fair-haired child. The house commanded a lovely view of the sea, and was surrounded by roses and geraniums in full bloom; otherwise we might have imagined ourselves in England, so thoroughly English was the tone of the household. We had a long, busy, delightful day at Gibraltar, driving about in Colonel ———'s pretty English carriage; and the very name of the place will always be pleasant to me on account of the wonders of nature and art we saw there, the brilliant atmosphere that made every impression doubly vivid, above all, the graceful and hearty hospitality of our host and hostess. Gibraltar is magnificent. Sorry, indeed, were we that we could not see it better and make it the head-quarters of excursions to Ronda, Tangiers, and Tetuan. As it was, we saw something of the stupendous galleries tunnelled in the rock, something of the bastions and batteries, something of the marvellous scenery from the heights, and something of the gay, rattling, picturesque town. We saw nothing of the apes—a little colony who have the topmost crags all to themselves, and are most religiously and wholly tabooed, no one being allowed to molest or kill them—and nothing of the three hundred classes of plants, which are said to flourish on the rock. Neither did we see anything of those picturesque Ronda smugglers whom Captain Scott describes so enthusiastically in his travels published nearly thirty years ago. But we saw enough of Gibraltar to leave it with regret and to look upon our last day in Spain—for I suppose I may so call it—as one of the brightest.

At nine o'clock gun-fire we left the port in an open boat, and after an hour's rowing reached our steamer, the *Spahis*. The night was glorious, and the sea as smooth as glass. Overhead shone myriads of large bright stars, and the lights of Gibraltar made a lesser, but hardly less brilliant, firmament lower down. We thought, as we looked alternately at those shining fields above and below, we had happy auspices for our onward journey.

CHAPTER XIII.

A BRIDAL PARTY.—HORRIBLE STORIES.— A LONG DAY.—THE CAID
AND THE DRIVER.—A NEW ATMOSPHERE.—TLEMCEN.

E had originally intended to take tickets for Oran, but finding that the *Spahis*, if weather permitting, stopped at a little town called Nemours, we resolved to stop there. By this plan we saved ourselves a day and a night at sea, and alighted at a point on the African coast much nearer Tclemcen than Oran. The weather favoured us. When we awoke next morning the sun shone bright and warm in a cloudless sky, and the steamer was gliding gently as a swan over the still, lake-like waters.

This sea-passage between Gibraltar and Oran is a dull one, and in our case it was especially so, as we were the only first-class passengers, excepting an old French gentleman, an *employé* of the Imperial Messagerie Company, who, with his son and daughter-in-law—a bride of a few days—was bound also to Nemours.

One great resource was a bundle of English newspapers kindly supplied to us at Gibraltar, and we pored over them from morning till the early twilight, when there was a ringing of bells and a smell of dinner, and an air of liveliness among the little company on board.

I joined the *table d'hôte*, and found it very amusing. The captain had travelled all over the world, and had evidently made use of his eyes and ears everywhere, and the bridal party were by no means dull. After dinner the father-in-law ordered champagne, and the officers were invited in to drink the health of the little bride. She, poor child, was a little overcome, what with her new honour as Madame, sea-sickness, and the prospect of exile at Nemours; but all the rest were merry enough, and when we retired to our cabin we heard their talk and laughter till late in the night. There was not much time to sleep, for about three o'clock we were told to dress ourselves in readiness for the boat, and an hour later we went on deck. It was cold and fine. The sea was perfectly calm, but we heard it breaking on the shore with an angry, threatening sound, and we saw in the dim, grey light, what a rocky coast it was, and what a barrier there was, against which the smoothest sea could not break silently. Nemours is, indeed, no harbour, but a mere *rade*, and only approachable in the calmest weather, and by small boats. A hard pull our good boatmen had of it ere we could reach the landing-place, and the poor bride shivered in her thin summer dress.

" I was married in such a hurry," she had said to me, " that mamma had no time to prepare anything, and all my clothes are to be sent after me ;" but it seemed to me that a good warm shawl for the sea-journey would not have required much preparation. However, we wrapped her up in spare rugs and great-coats, and I think she took no harm.

We had to be carried ashore one at a time, and I thought of Gilliat, and of the sea-faring life Victor Hugo has portrayed so fantastically, when savage-looking men, their bare limbs shining like bronze in the pearly light, dashed into the water, and bore us to the strand as easily as if we were babies.

Much as we had enjoyed Spain, how glad we were to find ourselves in France again, especially in African France!—to find ourselves speaking, as it were, our native language, and not having to try at the stately Spanish phrase, to hear the friendly French voice, and see the friendly French faces around us, to know that wherever we went, we were really and truly welcome, and that we might do exactly as we liked without being thought extraordinary!

We found Nemours just like any other little French town in Algeria, very formal and neat, with a little square, a little church, and boulevards in their babyhood, and a certain indescribable air of order and importance about it. We went straight to the inn—I think it was called *l'Hôtel des Voyageurs*—and, after knocking once or twice, the landlord came down, very shaggy and sleepy, but pleasant and amiable, as Frenchmen always are. He went out at once to his neighbour, the baker's, and came back with a pan of red-hot ashes, which was very clever of him, for we were bitterly cold, and nothing else would so effectually have heated the room. Then he brought us out a bottle of good Bordeaux and excellent bread and Rochefort cheese; and by the time we had finished our meal, there was a clean bedroom ready for us and hot water: and what more does a weary traveller require? The *douane* did not choose to wake up and give us our luggage till late in the morning; it was such a lazy *douane;* and though I went again and again, and said pretty things to the gendarmes, it was of no use. They said pretty things in return, but kept the luggage. At last the *douane* chose to wake up and open its doors, and we got our portmanteaus, and were able to get at brushes and combs and clean dresses, and to sit down to breakfast clothed and in our right minds.

Then we obtained the services of an old soldier as guide, and went out to see something of Nemours. The weather was perfect, and our guide just the person to make you feel in a new world. He had something unexpected to tell us about everything; the people of Nemours, the past of

Nemours, and the present aspect of French-African colonization collectively.

A bright blue sea, glistening white sands, and bold dark rocks, will make any place beautiful; but, otherwise, Nemours is uninteresting enough. It is only when you are outside the town, and breathing the air of the wild desolated hills, that you understand the romance of the place. For the history of Nemours, if written with a vigorous pen, would abound in incidents as thrilling as any conceived by the author of *Monte Christo*, or of *The Last of the Mohicans*.

We passed through the town, and were just entering upon a picturesque gorge, when our guide pointed to a little farm-house that peeped sunnily from its orchards and gardens, and said,—

" Do you see a great patch of new whitewash, just above the door yonder?"

" Yes, we see it."

" *Eh, bien!* I will tell you the history of that patch of new whitewash. A good colonist lived in that house, and was murdered a few weeks back by the Arabs. He went to bed as usual, first having seen that every lock was secure, and that his pistol was loaded—for only fools go unarmed here by night or day—and at midnight woke suddenly, hearing the dogs bark and the cocks crowing. 'The Arabs!' he says to his wife, who wakes up too, and then he takes up his pistol and throws open the window, ready to scare the scoundrels away. But before he can do it, he is shot through his head, and his blood and brains are all over the wall, and so it had to be whitewashed as you see."

"And the poor widow, and the guilty Arabs?"

"The widow lives there still. The poor can't indulge in fine feelings, you see, Madame, and must stay where their bread is to be earned. The Arabs got away to Morocco—they can do it in a few hours from here—and *voilà l'histoire!*"

"A sad history indeed!"

"And not the saddest I could tell you. Ah! Madame, the life of us poor colonists here on the borders of Morocco is hard enough. Only the good God knows how to understand how hard it is" (*le bon Dieu sait seul comment c'est dur.*)

"On account of the great insecurity, you mean?"

"Yes, Madame. We have to keep watch-dogs

as fierce as tigers, to look well to our bolts and pistols before going to bed, to distrust an Arab as *le diable*, and, withal, we are always being burned out, robbed, assassinated; and those who burn us out, rob us, and assassinate us, as often as not get across to Morocco safe and sound."

" But the soldiers protect you?"

" Mon Dieu, Madame! the soldiers have hard work to protect themselves! and the soldiers, you see, are not always hand and glove with the colonists. I often think we should do better in Algeria without soldiers at all. Being a *colon* myself now, I speak for the *colons*, of course."

We were now in a wild and beautiful spot at some distance from the town. On either side rose green hills, sharply shutting in a little river that flowed amid tamarisk and oleander, and, here and there, shone the round white dome of some small Moorish sanctuary.

We sat down to rest a little while and enjoy the perfect solitude of the place, and sketch the nearest of the mosques or marabouts.

" Ah! that is a marabout which will never be forgotten as long as the French hold Oran. A few years ago there was sharp fighting in these parts, and the Arabs, who were very strong, contrived to get a few hundred of our brave fellows here by some diabolical cunning or other, and, being thousands themselves, mowed them down like so much standing corn. But this is only one story of hundreds. If blood of the bravest would make lands rich, we ought to have fine crops here, indeed, Madame."

"The Arabs seem a very savage set here," one of us said. "Around Algiers they are, for the most part, harmless."

"*Il y a des Arabes et des Arabes. Voilà*, Madame. We are close on Morocco. The Arabs who have burned, murdered, and stolen in other places flee hither, and so we are in a sort of Botany Bay of 'em."

Just as he spoke a wild figure came running down the mountain side, and made towards us, gesticulating, crying aloud, shaking his shaggy hair, laughing a horrible laugh. So brown he was, and so uncouth an object, that it seemed belying alike Frenchman and Arab to class him as either. Instinctively we started and drew back.

"Don't be alarmed, ladies," said our old soldier, with a smile; "it's only a poor madman—he is harmless enough if not teazed. *Bon soir, bon soir, Père Michie, ça va bien; tu vas te promener? C'est ça. Allons!*" And the poor creature mouthed and laughed and went his way. This was the only person we met in that solitary walk. When we returned, the short, bright day was drawing to a close, and we were so tired that we were even glad to lie down and shut out the glorious colours that spread in fiery flakes across the sky, and the purple sea, that seemed like another firmament in its immovableness and depth, and the large pale stars that seemed to belong to both.

The stars were not pale when we arose next morning at three o'clock to start for Tclemcen; it was worth one's while to rise at that hour, if only to see them, so large and brilliant and wonderful were they; and shining out of heavens, neither blue, nor purple, nor black, but indescribably beautiful. Never shall I forget that journey from Nemours to Tclemcen. The day seemed interminable. First of all, we had the long, long reign of stars,—stars that dazzled like suns, mildly luminous, moonlike stars, and pale, primrose-coloured stars, that trembled and heralded the dawn. Then we had the dawn,—a long, grey, cold dawn that seemed a day in itself, and then the blessed sun, warming the day into perfect ripeness, as if it were a flower, and then the twilight again, with new stars.

But if the longest day of our lives, it was by no means the least pleasant. The weather, as usual (for, I think, in point of weather, travellers were never so fortunate as ourselves!), was all that could be desired, warm, breezy, and bracing, and there was recreation for heart and brain in the region through which we passed. Every feature and aspect of the country was new to us. We had never before seen anything like these undulating wastes of sand, and these interminable plateaux of stone and grass, all bathed in the mellowest, warmest, most golden light. The light was one long surprise to us. We looked up at some sheep browsing on a rocky ledge, and they seemed turned into copper images of sheep; and not the mere white woolly things they are generally figured to be. We looked from a bit of rising ground across a broad steppe of sand and stone, and we could hardly believe that the sun was not setting, so yellow it was, and so full of misty, delicious warmth. Everything seemed transfigured, and the transfiguration was almost blinding. We were alone in the coupé of the diligence, and the only passenger in the rotunda was a stately Caïd, magnificently dressed in purple gaudoura and white bernous of softest, silkiest Algerian manufacture. But what was the magnificence of his dress to the magnificence of his complexion? To understand what an Arab complexion is, one must have seen it, as we saw it, bronzing and glowing under a southern sky. Transported to canvas or cold climates, the rich hue loses half its life and warmth and beauty.

When we alighted, the Caïd invariably alighted too, and he would smile down grandly upon us, as if we were children, and say a complacent word or two in broken French, as if he thought we were afraid of him. We were sorry enough that we could not talk with him, and tell him how far we had come to see the great works of the Moors in Spain and Tlemcen. Our driver was as picturesque as the Caïd, and almost as silent.

I think he was a Breton by his style of face, which was full of character and nobility, and such as Rembrandt would have painted. He wore a fur cap, very rich in colours, and a light blue coat of quaint shape, bordered with the same sort of fur. Anything finer or more poetic than this man's appearance, I had never seen. But, beyond the courtesy of offering us some of his wine, when we asked for water, he hardly opened his lips.

For the most part, the country was uncultivated and uninhabited. There was no foliage excepting that of stunted olive, tamarisk, and palmetto, and nothing to break the universal monotony but here and there a *douar*, or Arab village, consisting of a cluster of tents, hedged in by walls of wild cactus, or haulm. Whenever we passed close to such a douar, the dogs would rush out yelling and barking, the whole little brown-skinned community would come to the road-side and stare us out of sight. The younger children were generally naked, though such a brown skin seems a sort of clothing in itself, and the elder ones had nothing on but one *cutty-sark*, of coarse sacking or woollen stuff. The men and women were decently clothed, and would greet us with a grave "Salamalek!" or "Bon jour!" whilst the children, veriest imps of fun and impudence, ran after the carriage, begging for a sou as long as their breath would carry them.

We reached Tclemcen about six o'clock, and established ourselves at the Hôtel de France, a cool, pleasant, roomy house, where they gave us large rooms and Algerian fare, and gracious Algerian courtesy. We could willingly have stayed at Tclemcen for months.

CHAPTER XIV.

TCLEMCEN.—THE GRANADA OF THE WEST.—ARAB POETS.—
CHILDREN.—THE MOKBARA.—MANSOURA.—PHILO-ARABES.—
TEMPTATIONS TO TCLEMCEN.

AT Tclemcen, we found ourselves in a second and hardly less beautiful Granada —a Granada moreover peopled with those who had made it what it was, a Granada not wholly dead, but teeming with happy, picturesque Eastern life. The climate is delicious, and the whole atmosphere of the place so gracious and sweet to live in, that one is never ready to come away. We made up our minds to stay a week or ten days in this Capua of Capuas, whose climate, scenery, and every element around us, gave wings to the hours. We never knew how the time went; we only know that, like Faust, we said to the hour, "Stay, for thou art fair," and that it escaped us like a vision. For those who wish to know what Tclemcen, the "Queen of Marreb" (in Morocco), really is, and was, I refer them to the beautiful and careful papers of M. Brosselard in the *Revue Africaine*. If I were to say half what I want to say about Tclemcen, this little book would swell into a big one; I will, therefore, do my utmost not to be enthusiastic, since enthusiasm leads me into the rash use of so many words.

The Arabs, who are enthusiastic about great things and small, have described Tclemcen in language as brilliant as a bed of tulips. Listen, for instance, to Abd-el-Kader, who made Tclemcen his capital after the treaty of Tafna in 1837: "At sight of me," says the great poet, "Tclemcen gave me her hand to kiss; I love her as the child loves the bosom of his mother. I raised the veil which covered her face, and my heart palpitated with joy; her cheeks glowed like flames. Tclemcen has had many masters, but she has showed indifference to all, turning from them with drooping eyelids; only upon me has she smiled, rendering me the happiest sultan in the world; she said to me, 'Give me a kiss, my beloved; shut my lips with thy lips, for I am thine.'"

Another Arab writer thus describes Tclemcen: "Tclemcen is a city enjoying a pleasant climate, running waters, and a fertile soil. Built on the side of a mountain, it reminds one of a fair young bride reposing in beauty on her nuptial couch. The bright foliage which overshadows the white roofs is like a green coronal circling her majestic brow. The surrounding heights and the plain stretching below the town are made verdant by running streams. Tclemcen is a city that fascinates the mind and seduces the heart." Thus wrote in the 15th century Ibn Khaldoun, the Arab Prescott, whose work no one has completed; and though the sun of Tclemcen has set, it is so beautiful as to fascinate the mind and seduce the heart still.

It was under the bright, brief dynasty of the Abd-el-Ouadites that Tclemcen was virtually the Queen of Morocco. Possessed of a large, enlightened, and wealthy population, of commercial enterprise, of a well-disciplined army, a brilliant court, munificent and cultivated rulers, Tclemcen was one of the best governed and most polished capitals in the world, as her monuments bear witness.

If you go farther back into history, you find Tlemcen was christened "Pomaria" by the Romans, on account of its orchards and fruit-gardens, but the Tlemcen of to-day is far more interesting. It is indeed the Moorish Athens. The modern city lies at the foot of green hills, its minarets standing out against the sky, its terraced houses surrounded by belts of lustrous foliage, whilst beyond stretches a plain as grandly covered with ruins as the seven hills of Toledo ; only unlike the hills of Toledo, green, and sunny, and gay.

The life of the streets is intoxicating to an artist. At every corner you see children playing, as brightly dressed as little Prince Bedreddin when he went with his slave to buy tarts ; the boys wearing blue and crimson vests, embroidered with yellow braid, scarlet Fez caps, and spotlessly white trousers ; the girls, such dainty, dark-eyed darlings! in soft white dresses and haïks, their waists bound with broad silk scarfs of many colours, and flowers stuck coquettishly behind their little ears. Never were such children as those of Tlemcen, so pretty, so frolicsome, so utterly kittenish and captivating. You could not help stopping to play with them; one would like to adopt half-a-dozen of them as nephews and nieces. The Negro and Jewish children are also very pretty here. The Jewesses brighten the streets as much as the children. They are handsomer here than in Algiers, and wear outside their brocades and silks haïks of soft, bright crimson cloth, which envelope them from head to foot. The Arab type is handsomer too; I should say much purer. There was a boy of fifteen at the hotel whose face I shall never forget. It was the face one should copy for a Christ in the Temple; perfectly oval, the features refined and pensive; the eyes soft, dark, and full of expression; the mouth sweet and serious. This boy acted as our guide, and as soon as we had arranged our sketch-books and shawls, would lose himself in a reverie. His face then was perfect.

We used to divide our days between the Arab village of Sidi Bou Medin and the mines of Mansooua.

The way to Sidi Bou Medin lies amid one vast cemetery called the *Mokbara*, where the Tclemcenites have been buried for hundreds of years. A

French guide-book has this remark upon the horrible condition of this cemetery,—"Ici s'amoncellent depuis des siècles les tombes des Tclemcéniens ; le temps les a peu respectés :" but is it time alone that has so mishandled the dead?

There was hardly a spot where time (or the road-maker ?) had not laid bare some skeleton, and in some places the bones lay in heaps. Some pretty little Marabouts lie scattered about these acres of grave-yard, and near one we saw a ragged Bedouin at afternoon prayer. The kneeling man, the white temple peeping amid olive-trees, the long lines of the cemetery, the yellow evening light bathing all, made a touching picture. The dry bones preached to us. We thought of the Moors driven thither from Spain, and of the sad hearts they brought into exile.

The village of Sidi Bou Medin covers a hill terrace-wise, and is overtopped by a graceful minaret. It has a gracious and sunny aspect, with its hanging gardens of myrtle, and orange, and pomegranate, its running streams, its vineyards and olive-groves, its shining white domes and minarets. Not a French element has entered the place; and when we had climbed the precipitous shady path and entered the court of the great Mosque, we felt as far from France as if Abd-el-Kader's dream of a new Mahomedan dynasty at Tlemcen were realised, and the Nureddin was summoning, not Bedouins and beggars only, but turbaned princes and rulers to prayer.

Sidi Bou Medin, from whom the village is called, was a great saint, and his tomb (*koubba*) is considered the sight to see, it being very richly decorated with draperies of cloth and gold, ostrich's eggs set in silver, chains and amulets of gold and beads, arabesques, mirrors in mother-of-pearl frames, lustres and lamps. To enter this *koubba*, you first descend into a little court, around which runs a graceful arcade supported on pillars of onyx; the panels are decorated with inscriptions, and hung with cages of singing birds, and the whole place is wonderfully rich and fantastic.

The Arabs heap up wealth on the shrines of their favourites with a zeal unequalled by Romanists, however fervent, and Bou Medin is the favourite saint here. There are many strange, touching, and also—for even saints have humour

—comic stories about him. He was born in Spain, and was brought up, first to arms, then to the profession of science; but, after many wanderings to Cordova, to Bagdad, to Mecca, to Constantine, came to Tlemcen, finding it, as he said, "a place in which the eternal sleep must be sweet," where he died with these noble words on his lips,—"God alone is the Eternal Truth."

His life, as are all the lives of Mahomedan saints, was meditative and active, miraculous and ordinary, and abounds in legends. He could read the most secret thoughts of men, in testimony of which the Arabs tell this story:—"A certain Sheikh was angry with his wife, and wishing to be separated from her, without feeling quite sure that he had reasonable grounds for doing so, went one day without saying a word to anybody to consult Sidi Bou Medin. Hardly, however, had he entered the room when the Marabout looking at him, called out sharply,—

"'Fear God, and don't put away your wife!'

"Of course the Sheikh was at a loss to understand how the saint came to quote the Koran so à propos, to which Sidi Bou Medin replied,—

"'When you came in, I saw, as it were, the words of the Koran written on your person, and I guessed at once what was in your mind.'"

From the court you enter the *koubba* itself. The cenotaph, which is of richly sculptured wood, lies under a dusky dome, only lighted by small panes of coloured glass. A blessed disciple and friend of the saint lies by his side.

But it is the beauty of the mosque that those who are not devotees at Sidi Bou Medin's shrine, care most to look at. Here you see *azulejos* and *artesonados* as original in design and as perfect in finish as any in Grenada, and probably of the same period. The tiles of the three primary colours, red, yellow, and blue, within, the sculptured red tiles without, the sculptured porticoes and walls, are quite of the same style, and in no degree unequal to the finest Moorish work we had seen in Spain. There are intact some of those gorgeous inscriptions, historical and religious, such as crowd the seat of the Caliph in the mosque of Cordova, and I do not remember to have seen any defacement or dilapidation anywhere. The building is a perfect specimen of Moorish art, which is always simple where simplicity has its use, and always profuse of ornament, where ornament is in place. Take, for instance, the outer court where the Arabs perform their ablutions before prayer; there you have a marble basin, a floor of *faïence* in bright colours, all shut in by an airy arcade and overhead a bright blue sky. What could you add that would not spoil the purpose of the place?— a purifying place that ought to be unadorned. But within, where the devout man has the right to worship, having purified himself, flesh and spirit by the outward and visible sign as well as the inward and spiritual grace, the Mahomedan makes his temple magnificent for the one God and His Prophet. Neither wealth nor workmanship is spared, and the result is what we see, walls covered with ornamentation, most delicate both as to colour and design, pillars of jasper and onyx, arcades of lovely fret-work, the priestly seat or pulpit of cedar-wood richly sculptured—lavishness of labour and perfection of form and colour everywhere.

The ruins of Mansourah, once the rival of Tclemcen, lie about two miles off the town. It is now six centuries since this city was one vast congeries of palaces, public buildings, gardens, baths, hospitals, and mosques. Nothing remains now but ruined walls and the minaret, though these alone are quite sufficient to show what Mansourah once was.

Photographs might help you a little to imagine the place, but, having looked at them, you must shut your eyes and colour the minaret and the walls with richest, reddest ochre, you must clothe the hills in living green, fill the space between hill and sky with soft warm skies of southern blue, and then set the whole picture floating and palpitating in golden mist.

This minaret is unlike anything else in the whole world. It is like a gigantic monolith of solid Indian gold, and is as wonderful as the Pyramids. When you come closer you see what a ruin it is now, and what a splendour it once was; it has been cleft in two like a pomegranate. The construction is of a rich reddish-coloured tile, and these tiles are arranged in panels sculptured and coloured. Some of the colour remains wonderfully bright still, but the whole building would hardly stand the shock of an earthquake,

I think. Looking at the inner side, you see the traces of inclined stairs by which mounted horsemen could ride to the top, and by dint of a little patience, you are able to master the original ground-plan of the place. The exquisite columns of jasper and marble have been removed to the museums of Tclemcen, Algiers, and Paris, where are also to be seen many beautiful mosaics, enamelled tiles, shafts, and pedestals.

Whilst sitting at the foot of this minaret and looking from one scene of ruin to another, we found some fragments of coloured glass, blue, green, amber and red, which alone sufficed to show how splendid the mosque must have been. We looked at these bits of broken glass which were brilliant as jewels, and from them to the half-buried portico and the shattered minaret; and gradually the past became vivid as a dream, the dry bones were covered with flesh, the flesh palpitated with happy life, and the city of Mansourah was young and fair and gay again!

But we did not live wholly in the Tclemcen of yesterday. There is quite a little Protestant colony here, and we found ourselves taking up threads of interests long laid aside, and here, in a remote corner of Africa, discussing all those questions dear to the well-wisher of the English Church. We talked naturally a good deal of the Arabs and discovered that we were in a nucleus of what French writers on Algerian affairs call *Philo-Arabes*. One gentleman, a German, I think, but of whatever nation a most intelligent person, worked himself into quite a passion of indignant eloquence.

"I assure you, Madame," he said, "that much as I love Tclemcen, and well as my affairs are thriving here, I do not know how to stay. The treatment of the Arabs enrages me—who am a peaceable man—fifty times a-day. You will hear wherever you go that the Arab is a sensual, unprincipled wretch, given to slaying, stealing, and all kinds of vice. You must not believe half what you hear, Madame; I have lived long enough among the Arabs to know what they are, and this is what they are,—harmless, generous, patient, hospitable, religious; they are all this and often much more. If I go from Tclemcen to Oran, do you think I want a pistol? Madame, I need never bear the expense of going to an hotel; every Arab tent or house is open to me; at any man's table I am welcome to a meal; his children will play with me; his own sons will tend or saddle my horse; at parting he will wring my hands and bid me come again."

"We don't hear such things from everyone," we said.

"Ay, because you have doubtless had more talk with the soldier rather than the civilian, the ruler of the Arab than his fellow-man. But when a Colonel, or a Major, or a *Chef du Bureau Arabe*, tells you how wicked the Arabs are, and how necessary it is to beat them (*leur donner coups de bâton*), he does not tell you all the story, Madame. He does not tell you how there are some who make their fortune by bleeding the poor Arabs, and then go back to Paris to live grandly. He does not tell you how he administers justice, and that is worth your while to hear. I am a *Chef du Bureau Arabe,* so we will suppose, and I want something, no matter what,—a few jackal-skins for my wife's drawing-room, a little money, sheep, horses, anything. What do I do? The Arabs have all these things, skins, money, cattle, so I call my Sheikhs together, and tell them what I want, and they get it: what do I care how? and then people wonder that the Arabs rob in their turn! I tell you, Madame, that the Arab is unfairly treated in every way, and that those who treat him so will suffer for it hereafter. He would assimilate with us if we would only let him. To-day, for instance, I met a friend of mine, an Arab who lives in Tclemcen, and I told him that I would bring some English travellers to see his pretty Moorish house. He was as delighted as if he had been a countryman of yours. 'I will prepare a *diffa* (feast),' he said; 'there shall be a good *cous-cous-son* to regale your friends,' and if you go, you will find him, in every sense, a gentleman—polished, kindly, and intelligent. Our boys play together. Do you suppose those young Bedouins will not be influenced by the companionship? If I were to leave Tclemcen to-morrow, there are some Arabs I should part from as from my brothers."

"And then," said his young wife, treating the subject from a romantic point of view, "there is something so poetic about everything they do! If you ask a simple question, they answer you with parables and figures of speech. It is like reading the Scriptures. Oh, Madame! my husband is right in advocating the cause of the poor Arabs! I think they would teach us Christians many a lesson of piety and resignation. If a parent loses his child he says, 'It is the will of Allah. Allah's will be done!' The name of God is ever in their mouths, and I do believe in their hearts."

We heard a great deal more about the Arabs during our stay, and, curiously enough, every one here spoke hopefully of them. I could write a long chapter of the stories that were told us by these warm *Philo-Arabes*, but they carry double weight when told with flashing eyes and trembling lips. One hardly knows what to believe.

There are a good many Jews at Tlemcen, and it is consolatory to find them—as indeed you find them all over Algeria—living happily among their former enemies. The French conquest has certainly done a great deal for the Jews, who, under the Turkish rule, suffered inexpressible persecutions and hardships. Now they thrive, and thrive deservedly, without any fear that their honestly earned gains will be snatched from them, or that their derelictions will receive harsher punishment than those of their Christian neighbours.

If any one wants to renew his health, or forget his troubles, let him come to North Africa, and breathe the sweet, biblical, sunny atmosphere of Tclemcen. You will find no more tourists there than you would do in the heart of the Great Sahara; and whilst you enjoy all the charm of romantic, isolated Eastern life, none of the material comforts of modern civilization are missing.

CHAPTER XV.

HOSPITABLE ORAN.—CHRISTMAS DAY AT LE SIG.—THE LAST OF THE PHALANSTERIANS. — BARRAGES. — THE MALARIA.—ABD-EL-KADER'S MOSQUE.—SAÏDA.

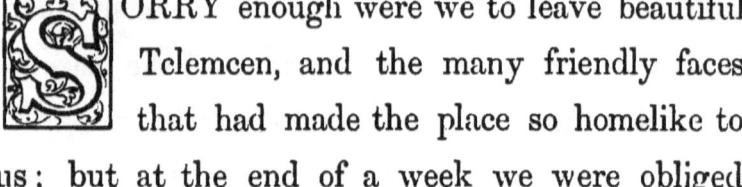ORRY enough were we to leave beautiful Tclemcen, and the many friendly faces that had made the place so homelike to us; but at the end of a week we were obliged to turn our faces towards Oran.

The diligence—wretched diligence!—travelled of course at night, and we set off for Oran in the evening, reaching our destination early next day, and not our destination only, but our welcome letters, newspapers, and books, luxuries of which we had been long deprived. Oran is a second and more bustling Algiers, only that Algiers is far more picturesque and Eastern. In Oran you are wholly in France—African France that is—with a burning blue sky in December, and a burning blue sea reaching to the foot of the town—if it were only cool enough to walk so far!

We kept indoors almost all day during our stay in Oran, resting ourselves after the hard travel gone before, and in anticipation of the hard travel to come. But we were as gay as possible; for what with letters of introduction from friends and friends' friends, we had visitors all day long, and invitations for every evening. Certainly hospitality flourishes on Algerian soil. It was quite delightful to be so welcomed and so regretted, and I cannot think of Oran without wishing to go there again—if life were long enough—just to shake hands and exchange an hour's talk with the kind and pleasant people whose acquaintance I made there.

Amongst other acquaintances we found during our short stay at Oran was that of M. Leon Beynet, whose "Drames du Désert," and other stories of African life, give one an admirable idea of the relative positions of native and colonist, Arab and Frank. M. Beynet makes the heroine of one of his stories a beautiful young Kabyle girl, who is certainly the most charming little savage that ever went unwashed. These novels are quite a feature in Algerian literature, and make you live in the wild scenes and society they portray.

Oran is a handsome city. The houses are of enormous height, and are built in blocks, so that the town is divided, so to say, into many parts. From each side of the city rise green hills and rocky heights, crowned by round white towers built by the Spaniards; and below lies the beautiful sea, so calm and blue during those December days, that we could hardly credit the bad weather written of from home. We had some pleasant walks on the hills, which abound in wild flowers, and everything else dear to the naturalist; but we were impatient to be making the best of our way Algiers-wards, and did not stop at Oran more than a few days.

Our next halting-place was Le Sig, where we spent Christmas-day. I doubt whether Le Sig would be found on any map, and I should not mention it except for an amusing error into which we were led respecting its claims upon our attention. "By all means go to Le Sig," people had said to us. "What, not go to Le Sig! The Phalansterian colony; the little community of Enfantinists and Fourierists!" So, as Le Sig lay on our way, we made a halt there, and saw what was to be seen.

Sig Proper is a prosperous little half French, half Spanish town, but Sig Phalansterian is a farm about a mile off; so as we reached the former at night we put up there, and found ourselves tolerably well off. The people were Spanish, and the cooking Spanish; whilst in Oran we were constantly coming upon such little clusters of Spanish families, who seemed thriving and happy.

Early next morning, we got a little Arab to show us the way to *La Colonie*, as the farm of the Phalansterians is called, and after a hot and dusty walk of half an hour, reached a rather deserted-looking homestead, consisting of farm-houses and buildings surrounded by orchards and vegetable gardens. This was the Phalanstery; but, alas! where was the spirit that should have animated the place? Where were the philosophical grinders of corn, and assiduous cultivators of the beautiful? where were the hives of children happier at their work than our children at their play? Nothing remains now of

T

all this; and instead of devout followers of Enfantin in broad-brimmed white hats, we saw ordinary French labourers working after the ordinary way. The Phalanstery has, in fact, dwindled down till only two of the original occupants are left, and these, Monsieur and Madame B——, are a simple, old-fashioned couple, who seem to concern themselves mighty little with Fourierism, let out such of the land as they do not care to farm themselves, and send their only child, a girl of twelve, to a convent school. It seemed impossible to believe that only a few years back this isolated spot was the centre of a fervid, determinate little community, who had fled thither from the storms and passions of the world, intending to plan a perfect life.

Monsieur and Madame B—— received us kindly, and took us all round the premises, showing us the former dwellings of the Phalansterians, neat little wooden houses in rows, now turned into stables and granaries. The *jardin potage* seemed very flourishing, and, indeed, so did the crops of every kind. We tasted the home-grown and home-made wine, but that was sour enough to have driven away the most ardent Fourierist going.

We had brought other letters to Le Sig, and by one of them were introduced to a charming young English lady, Madame O——, who had spent all her life in Africa, and was now settled down at Sig. Her husband was a Frenchman, and held an official post of some authority there, being entrusted with the supervision of the gigantic *barrages*, or water-works, which are turning the barren plain of Le Sig into gardens of beauty and fruitfulness.

When the Emperor was at Algiers, he asked some great authority on Algerian affairs what was most needed in the colony.

"Barrages, sire," was the answer.

"Et après cela?"

"Encore barrages," repeated the political economist; and the Emperor gave heed to the words, as those who follow in our track from Oran to Algiers will see. These gigantic and noble works are well worth inspection, especially at Le Sig; and if future travellers have the good fortune that fell to our share, they will come away with a very clear idea of the importance and working of these monster systems of irrigation. Monsieur O—— most kindly drove us to the *barrages* himself, and told us, in round numbers the annual cost of the works and the quantity of water dispensed; but I am afraid of quoting figures from memory, especially when they come to millions, and refer the curious reader to statistical reports.

The reservoirs are colossal. You drive through a pleasant and verdant country, part cultivated, part pasture, and then come to the entrance of a wild gorge, above which rises the colossal mass of masonry, like a sentinel guarding the vast tracts beyond. The burning African sun shone straight down upon the broad surface of the reservoir, turning the hard grey of the granite to a soft and beautiful orange colour. One might have thought the place a thousand years old. Whilst we rested here to sketch a little, a grave Arab with three little girls came up to look at us. The little girls had complexions the colour of ripe chestnuts, and were as wild and fearless as monkeys, dancing to the very edge of the stone platforms in a way that made us sick. There was no sort of coping, and we were some hundred feet above the river bed.

Next to the extraordinary and monkey-like

agility of these children, I was struck by their obedience. The father had but to knit his brow, to lift his finger, or to cry Ayesha, or Zorah, or Zaida, and these wild creatures obeyed like soldiers. Yet they did not seem one whit afraid of him, playing hide-and-seek behind the folds of his burnouse, caressing his hands, smiling up into his face.

When we had seen enough of the *barrages*, we went back to the town and spent a little time with Madame O—— and her children—half French, half English children, with Saxon skins and hair, and dark brown eyes, and speaking a pretty language of their own, mixed English, Arabic, and French. The house was very large, and stood embosomed in Eastern shrubberies; the orange, the oleander, the magnolia, the palm, and the almond; Arab servants in handsome dresses were lounging about the hall, and the whole made a pretty picture to bring away from the remote country of Le Sig. Madame O—— looked as fresh as a rose, but the children were a little fragile, and she told us how much they had suffered from malaria.

"The fever is the curse of the place," she said,

"and every one falls victim to it in turn. A few months back my husband was brought to death's door by it, and the poor children suffer frightfully. Ah! what should we do but for that blessed, blessed quinine!"

Wherever we went, we heard the same complaints. The fever—the fever—every one was ill, or had been ill, or was falling ill of the fever. We were particularly warned from exposing ourselves to the smell of freshly-ploughed soil. The earth seems to emit a sort of poison, and there is no remedy for the evil—which is felt by thousands—save planting and drainage. The only wonder is that colonisation has prospered in these districts at all; especially when you consider that there are other scourges, hardly less insupportable, such as locusts and Arab incendiaries.

From Le Sig we journeyed—always by diligence, to Mascara, a town that will always have a romantic interest as the birthplace of Abd-el-Kader.

Mascara is charming. Great chalk hills, each crowned with its little mosque or marabout, rise round the town, and, when you have climbed these hills, you come upon broad belts of half wild, half cultivated country, flanked with settlers' huts or Arab tents. The colouring of the place is thoroughly Eastern; you get here, as in Andalusia, long lines of wild cactus and aloe standing out against a burning blue sky, and those indescribable effects of yellow and white that are only seen where every building is whitewashed and every bit of ground is toasted and bronzed and baked by a blazing sun.

The place itself is quite French, and herein we were a little disappointed, as we had been led to expect a second Tclemcen, bright as Joseph's many-coloured coat, with Moorish costume. The Arab population is a very shabby one, and is, for the most part, settled outside the town, in wretched huts built of cob and rubble. We went inside the mosque, now used as a granary, where Abd-el-Kader preached war against the Christians, and found it very pretty, but in sad ruin. There were formerly beautiful tiles and arabesques on the walls, not a trace of which remains. Nothing, indeed, remains, but the beautifully-proportioned domes and aisles and the ceiling of inlaid cedar-wood.

From Mascara we made an excursion to Saïda, where we smelt the real air of the Desert, and saw many wonderful things that must be described without hurry. Finding that the diligence to Saïda possessed neither coupé nor berlina, we engaged the whole vehicle to ourselves, and what a concern it was! The glass was out of the windows, the seats were rickety, the floor screeched ominously whenever we got in or out. Never was such a crazy old diligence in the world, and, as we went along, it had spasmodic attacks of creaking and cracking without any rhyme or reason, and we expected nothing more nor less than a total collapse in some wild spot or other—which, however, did not happen.

It takes a day to get from Mascara to Saïda, but not a long day. If there were only tolerable roads and saddle-horses, the journey would be trifling. As it is, you are shaken up and down in a way that turns you sick and blackens and bruises you, and, though a halt of five minutes and a breath of the sweet air of the Desert revives and heals, you get to Saïda tired enough. What added to our discomfort was a high wind that accompanied us all the way, first making us shiver with cold, and afterwards burning us with a sirocco-like heat. We did our best to keep out the alternate cold and heat, but it was difficult work as all the windows were broken. As soon as one improvised curtain was up, another was sure to be down; and at last we solved the difficulty by covering our faces instead. I think the journey to Timbuctoo could hardly be wilder or more solitary than this. For the most part we passed through a totally uninhabited country—some parts all stone and sand; others overgrown with rosemary, wild asparagus, fennel, candied tuft, thyme, and stunted tuya and tamarisk trees. When the dust did not blow, the air was very sweet and invigorating, and sometimes the sky looked suddenly cold and blowy, and we could walk in comfort. After passing a vast and beautiful plain we stopped at a little village or post to breakfast and change horses. It was a curious half French, half Arab sort of settlement; and from the Arab douar in the village close by came lots of little half naked children to look at us. When we had breakfasted we went up to the tents to sketch, and soon had an eager group round us,—a stately Bedouin, his wives, his mother, and their children. Every one wanted to be useful, to hold the umbrella or the palette, or fetch water; and, when nothing remained to do, they watched the artist with smiles of amazement and gratification. The grandmother was a delightful old lady. She was by no means ugly as most old Arab women are, but had quite a nice face with very bright eyes and very intelligent features. She had keen observation too, as I saw, for, without being in the least degree rude and troublesome, she looked at us so narrowly that she doubtless preserves to this day an exact remembrance of what we were, how we looked, and what we said, or what she thought we said to each other. I should like to have adopted that old lady as my grandmother and brought her to England. Her sympathy with the sketcher was quite beautiful, and, when the children giggled and tittered and came so close to her as to hinder her progress and bring forth some such expression as this—"How are we to send these troublesome little things away,"—the old lady understood at once and commanded them to be still, which they were;

and as the objects of the landscape were brought out one by one, the dark-brown tents, the bright blue sky, the wavy, yellow plain, the low line of purple hills beyond—she cried aloud in ecstacy.

Whilst we were so occupied, a little urchin of five years, utterly naked, ran out of the tent close by and stood still, as much amused with us as we were with him. All laughed aloud, but the father who looked a little ashamed, and I think it was because he had been to Mascara or some other town, and knew that nakedness was not quite the thing in the great world. The women were like big children, and giggled, showing their white teeth, if you but held up a finger.

When we had done we shook hands all round, and returned to the auberge to see a pitiful sight. It was a little Arab child of fourteen months old sick of the fever; he was riding on the shoulder of his grandfather, a patriarchal-looking old man, with silky white hair and beard. I don't think I ever saw anything more touching than his care of the little suffering thing. Its poor little face was perfectly livid, its eyes leaden, its limbs shrunken. What could we do for it?

The mistress of the auberge came out and questioned the old man in Arabic a little, then turned to us.

"Ah!" she said, "think of it—that poor baby has neither father nor mother, no one to tend it but that old man, and it has been ill of fever for months; but then we all suffer alike! Three of my five children are ill now; that is, ill every other day with shivering fits and sickness, and there is nothing to do but try quinine. But quinine is very dear, and we have to do without it."

"Do the Arabs try it?" I asked.

She shrugged her shoulders expressively.

"*Voyez-vous, madame*, the Arabs are poorer than we. We must buy bread before quinine."

We gave the poor old man a little money, and recollecting that I had brought a small bottle of quinine from England, fearing these marsh fevers myself, I got it out of my travelling-bag and gave it to the woman. She promised to give the poor baby a dose, but I fear he was past all help, and I looked sadly after the old man as he stalked away in his tattered burnouse, bearing his poor little burden on his shoulders.

Farther on, we stopped to see some hot springs which lie within a few leagues of Saïda. Following a small path that wound through labyrinthine thickets of tuya, palmetto, and lentisk, we came suddenly upon a scene, that with very little idealization might make as poetic a picture as one could see.

It was a party of Arab girls bathing in a small round pool. The bathers and the bathing-place were shut in by lustrous green foliage, above which showed the dark lines of the tents, the bright blue hills, and the brighter sky. A noontide shadow lay on the water, in which, like a flock of young ducks, plashed and played, and dived and ducked, a dozen wild young girls, their dark hair streaming to the waist, their faces expressive of the utmost enjoyment, their limbs glistening as they rose out of the water.

All at once they caught sight of us. There was a short succession of screams, a unanimous splashing, a glimpse of bare feet, and all was still again. They had fled the spot without even a thought of their clothes; and we unfortunate intruders were only harmless women after all!

After this we passed a tawny, monotonous region, all stone and sand, and only here and there varied by oases of cultivation. These little oases, poor patches of wheat and vegetables growing amid the intractable palmetto, were showing green and bright, despite the rudeness of the tillage; but, alas! the locusts had found them out. Both on our journey to Saïda and back we saw swarms of these creatures settling like glittering birds on the corn, or filling the air like snow-flakes. My heart sank within me as I thought of the poor Arabs and the devastation that threatened their little all.

We reached Saïda in good time that afternoon.

CHAPTER XVI.

OPINIONS, CIVIL AND MILITARY.—A LOOK TOWARDS THE SAHARA.—
WILD GEESE.—OUR SPAHIS, AND THE CARE THEY TAKE OF US.
—A NORMANDY APPLE-ORCHARD IN AFRICA.—NEW YEAR'S
DAY.

SOME authorities declare Saïda to be an oasis in the Little Desert, some declare it to be an oasis in the Great Desert, others declare it to be in no desert at all. For my part, I wholly side with those who are of opinion that Saïda stands on the skirts of the Sahara, the Dry Country abounding in Dates, as the old maps have it; but I will leave the matter an open question to the curious, merely describing Saïda as I found it.

We had a comfortable room in the house of our coachman—for as nobody ever goes to Saïda there are no inns—whose wife was Spanish, and as ugly and dull as he was handsome and bright. As he seemed devoted to her, however, it didn't much matter. They carried on almost as many trades as there are weeks in the year, and were evidently making money. They catered for the officers, they kept the diligence, they owned land, they had geese and cattle, they managed the post—it would be hard to say what they did not do. And they wore good clothes, lived on really dainty food, and were of importance in the place, which must have been some consolation under exile.

Our first thought was to inquire for horses and side-saddles, our second to forward our letters to the Commandant. The first request proved fruitless. There being no ladies at Saïda, how should there be ladies' saddles? But M. le Commandant very kindly came to us at once, and told us what to see and how to see it in this oasis, as he delighted to call Saïda. He was a merry, middle-aged gentleman from Normandy, who had seen a good deal of the Desert, and bore the responsibilities of his post— which were heavy—with great ease.

"The life here seems dull," he said, "but after long marches in the Desert and hard fighting, I assure you I am very contented to remain here. There isn't a lady in the place, *c'est vraiment triste ça*, but there is an infinity of distractions in the way of work and pleasure. You see I represent both civil and military authority, having 40,000 Arabs under my jurisdiction, and this involves all sorts of intricacies, out of which I make my way as well as I can. I have to act as military commander, mayor, and prêfet, all in one ; and these Arabs are difficult people to manage, I assure you."

"They are miserably poor, are they not?" we asked.

"*Pauvres diables!* You may well say that; Madame. They are starving ; that's just the truth of it ; and what with those who steal and murder because they are hungry, and those who steal and murder because they like it, the road from hence to Fig-gig—our last post in the Desert—is unsafe enough. Without a military escort it is impossible."

"We were told at Oran," I said, "that there were some grand waterfalls we could see in the neighbourhood of Saïda. Is the excursion practicable?"

M. le Commandant opened his eyes, and shrugged his shoulders expressively.

"Madame, no one knows in Oran what is going on at Saïda. It is not practicable. I tell you the simple truth when I say that. It is not practicable. I will tell you what you can see here. You propose to remain two days? *Eh, bien!* to-morrow I will send an escort of Spahis with you as far as the marabout of Sidi-ben-Baila, from whence you can look over the plateaux which commence the Desert; you will see then what sort of country it is; and if you went on as far as Géryville, our next post, and Fig-gig our last, you would see no more. The next day you would like to sketch, probably? *Bien*, I send my servant and a Spahi with you to the ravine, and you will find fine things to draw; and when my work is done, I will ride round and show you what else is to be seen in our little Saïda;" and, after telling us a great deal more that was interesting, the good-natured Commandant left us.

We carried out these plans, and all turned out satisfactorily. There was only one sort of vehicle to be had, a sort of wheel-barrow on four wheels, belonging to a butcher, which we gladly accepted for the drive to the marabout. Our driver, the owner of the cart, proved a most entertaining person. He was a Parisian by birth, an African by right of long residence, and as rich in mother-wit as an American.

"You don't mean to say that you think of leaving Saïda without going to see the waterfalls?" he asked; "why, that is the only thing that is really beautiful in the place."

We said that we had been dissuaded from the excursion on account of the unsafety of the roads; and, thereupon, the incredulity of the butcher's face was a sight to see.

"*Mon Dieu, Madame*, you mustn't listen to what the military authorities say—they always make mountains of mole-hills. I would undertake to carry you safe to Fig-gig in this trap without as much as a pistol in my belt. *Voilà!*"

"But you don't attempt to convince us that the roads are safe, do you?"

"Madame, they are safe for you or for me; but I wouldn't say as much for myself if I were an officer. This is how it is, the Arabs hate the military, and do them an ill turn when they can; but the Arabs, *ma foi*, are not the bad set of people one would have you believe. Why, I have travelled to Géryville and back, and to Fig-gig and back alone before now alone, with money in my purse too, and the Arabs treated me as if I had been a brother, made me a dish of cous-cous-sou, gave me a bed under their tents, saddled my horse for me at parting, and bade me God speed. Having been so kindly treated by the Arabs, can you wonder at my speaking so of them? For my part I don't see a pin to choose between a good Christian and a good Mahomedan, a bad Christian and a bad Mahomedan : *voilà ce que nous pensons.*"

We let our butcher have his way, for his talk was too racy and fresh to be spared in a world where one has to endure so much commonplace. I should fill a chapter if I were to repeat half the stirring stories and original opinions he gave us; but as this little book is intended as a stimulant to others longing "for the palms and temples of the South," I hope it may lead some to Saïda and the butcher's acquaintance.

All this time we were driving through what seemed to be a stony desert, flooded with an indescribably yellow, mellow, monotonous light, above all, a pale blue sky. By-and-by, we came to a rocky height where we halted to take in every feature and aspect of a wondrous scene. Below lay a billowy waste of plain upon plain; those nearest to us broken by Arab tents, or the shining dome of a marabout; those farthest off more solitary, vaster, grander, than the surface of an ocean without a sail. Where the plains ended and the sky began was a straight, continuous line; and we looked at this line, so suggestive of distance, and mystery, and unknown existence, till we longed to accept the butcher's offer, and, *coûte que coûte*, set off for Fig-gig, and the "Dry Country abounding in Dates!"

What fascinated us more than anything was the wonderful briskness, purity, and sweetness of the air. It seemed as if we never could have breathed real air before, and the experience was too delicious to describe. Softer and sweeter than the breath blown off Cornish moors when the heather is out, fresher and more invigorating than the sea-breezes one gets at Lowestoft pier on a bright September day; a whiff of this air of the Desert amply repays any hardships undertaken to obtain it. We felt as if we could never come away, as if we could never drink deeply enough of such precious, reviving, rejuvenating wine. The Commandant's high spirits and comely looks, the butcher's vivacity, the general look of briskness, physical and mental, among the people of Saïda, was accounted for. The sweet air of the Desert did it all. I think if I went to live at Saïda the great-grandchildren of those who read what I write about it now, might, if they journeyed thither, find me alive and hearty.

About half a mile from our point of view stood the little marabout which was to be our boundary mark, and, around it, we could see wreaths of white smoke curling from the dark brown tents, and horses and cattle feeding. Near to us were one or two wild-looking Bedouins keeping their sheep, which were marvellously transformed in the yellow light, their fleeces looking like bosses of bright, orange colour. Whilst resting thus, a serried line of wild geese slowly flew towards us, keeping a line like the German letter _L_ till out of sight.

"Now we shall have rain," said our driver. "One wants no weather-glasses at Saïda, I assure you."

What inventions of man does one want indeed at such a place as Saïda? Place any one of quick mental capacity anywhere out of the world, that is to say, out of the conventional, comfortable world of shops, railways, and penny newspapers, and how readily does he shift for himself. Such a man as this butcher of Saïda had as many interests in life as any of us in these days of social, literary, and political excitement; he was always solving some knotty point in Algerian political economy, or speculating how this or that natural feature of the country could be turned to account. He knew the geography, geology, and mineralogy of every rood; he could tell what birds lived in the air, what beasts haunted the wastes, what plants grew in the oases, and how the Arabs lived in the Desert. It was curious to find how much more he respected the Bedouin than the Spahis, and how lightly he esteemed the moral influence of the French upon the people they had conquered. "Where are our Spahis?" I asked, for we had never seen our escort all the way.

He smiled and pointed to a cluster of Arab douars at some distance.

"You can't see a little red speck among those tents, I dare say, Madame; but my eyes are used to looking a good way off, and I can. It is one of your precious Spahis, and he's just thinking as much of you as his wives out there whom he has gone to see. I know 'em, those Spahis; they like nothing better than to be sent *as escort* with travellers, for that means that they can pay a visit to their women, who begin to cook couscous-sou as soon as ever they see a red cloak in the distance. When your Spahis have eaten up everything that comes in their way and seen enough of their good ladies, they'll come home."

And true enough, just as we were approaching Saïda, our escort came galloping up, two as wild and fine-looking men as you could see, their scarlet cloaks flung over their shoulders, their dark handsome faces wrapped in white linen trimmed with camel's hair, their brown muscular arms bare to the elbow, their legs thrust in mocassins of crimson leather richly embroidered. They rode pretty little barbs, and sat upon their high-backed saddles with quite a royal air. Nothing in the world could be more picturesque or brilliant.

Saïda, that is to say, the Saïda of yesterday,—for the present settlement is entirely French,—was heroically defended by Abd-el-Kader, and, as we drove home, we saw the ruined walls of the old town and the deserted camp of the French soldiery. Throughout the entire province of Oran, indeed, you are reminded of Abd-el-Kader, whose career has a wild, sad, Saracenic pomp about it not at all in harmony with our present civilization.

The French garrison of Saïda consists now of 800 men; and they have sixteen pieces of cannon only. We saw no more of our driver after that day. The superb air and savage plenty of such places as Saïda seem to make people magnanimous, for he went off to Géryville next day, never concerning himself about being paid for his services; and we were constantly receiving little presents from some one or other during our stay, ostriches' eggs, beautifully polished stones, wild boars' horns, &c., &c.

Saïda is a land of Goshen in the matter of game, and there is plenty of sport too. Jackals, hyenas, wild boars, abound in these rocky wildernesses; there are also panthers and gazelles, though they are found rarer. If it were not for the hunt and the chase, what would become of the officers under exile?

Next day, M. le Commandant showed us his pretty garden, planted with apple-trees by way of recalling his native Normandy, and promising to be very beautiful by-and-by, when the rich tropical flowers should be out. Then he went with us to a very savage and splendid gorge called *La Source*. Here, issuing from a tiny aperture in the rock, a stream of clear, rapid water had cleft its way through the rich red heart of the mountain, and tossed and tumbled amid oleanders and tamarisks as far as the eye could reach. The rock, piled in lofty masses on either side, made natural ramparts to the little town of Saïda which lay a mile off, forming the haunts of wild beasts and birds and Arab thieves.

"I have placed sentinels here for several nights of late," said M. le Commandant, "for the Arabs are like the jackals and steal down at night to scavenge where they can. My Spahis will come here as soon as it is dusk, and this precaution I must take till the thief or thieves are caught."

"And what will be done to them?"

"*C'est très simple,*" replied M. le Commandant coolly. "Whoever comes down that pass at night gets a bullet through his head, that's all." On our looking a little shocked he added, smiling, "*Que voulez-vous? Il faut vous dire les choses comme elles sont.*"

It seemed that the harvests had been very bad of late and that the Arabs were driven to all sorts of desperation by hunger. Was there work for those who chose to do it, we asked of the Commandant?

"In plenty, I assure you—in great plenty, Madame; but the Arabs don't like work, and will rather starve. Give a Kabyle a field to plough or a house to build, and he'll do it as well as a

Frenchman, whilst an Arab or Bedouin, you understand, is only good for fighting and plunder."

"That is your opinion."

"That is my experience, Madame."

Thanks to the kindness of the Commandant, we came away from Saïda with a pretty comprehensive idea of the perplexities and responsibilities of his high post, and of the working of the military system of government in Algeria.

Next day, the last day of the year, we returned to Mascara, and had, if anything, a more trying journey than before; the wind was colder, the sun was hotter, the clouds dustier, and every one prophesied rain.

We spent New Year's day with some kind friends from Algiers, Monsieur D——, an army surgeon, and his wife. What a sumptuous breakfast we had! I do not mean sumptuous in the matter of dishes only, but in the matter of conversation, which was as piquant and full of flavour as the fare. Monsieur D—— and his wife were two of those happy mortals who are gifted with perpetual youth, coupled with a habit of quick and just observation. An hour's talk with them was like reading a very witty and very wise novel. Throughout the shifting scenes of their African life, they had naturally fallen in with all sorts of characters and conditions, and they gave us a lively picture of French society in Oran, touching on the follies, errors, and good things of it, with kindly satire.

"I will take you to see Madame la Générale," said our hostess, "for I don't suppose in any of your travels you have been introduced to a Moorish lady married to a French commanding officer. Now, our General's wife is one; and, though she does not speak French quite easily, you will find her in dress and manner quite a Parisian. They have four children, such little dark, handsome, wild things, and there is not one of them so fond of sweets as mamma! Moorish ladies, you know, almost live on sugar."

Madame la Générale had a cold, however, and could see no one, so we had to leave Mascara without personal intercourse with a Moorish lady turned Parisian. It was certainly a disappointment.

It was quite a gay day at Mascara. New Year's day is always gay in France, and so warmly

were we received by Monsieur and Madame D——
that we did not feel as if we could be so far from
home and in a spot so remote as Mascara! French
hospitality, at least as far as my experience of it
goes, is as genuine and gracious hospitality as any
in the world; and we were quite touched by the
way in which people thought of us and for us
wherever we went.

To give one instance out of many :—On the
eve of our departure from Mascara, I was disturbed
in my packing by a gentle rap at the door, and on
opening it saw Monsieur D—— followed by an
Arab servant bearing a small basket heavily laden.

"Ah, Mademoiselle!" he said, "I disturb you—
but only for a little moment, and then I will wish
you '*bon voyage*' for the last time, and go.
When you and Madame had left us to-day, we
remembered that you praised my wife's preserved
peaches and apricots, and we thought you might
like some to eat on the way."

Then he helped his boy Hamed to unload the
basket, which contained several tin cases of fruit
hermetically sealed. I thanked him, said it was
too bad of us to rob Madame when she had been at

the trouble of preserving the fruit herself, that we should take the cases to England, that we should never forget the kind reception we had met at Mascara, &c.

"And we shall not forget," he said, with a hearty shake of the hand, "what pretty things you have said about French ladies in your book of Algerian travel! *Adieu, au revoir, Mademoiselle;* if not in Africa, in Paris; if not in Paris, in England!" and then he went.

We were to rise very early next morning, but, though we went to bed at eight o'clock, sleep was out of the question. New Year's Day only happens once a-year, and the good people of Mascara seemed determined to make the best of it. I never heard anything like tke noisiness of that little town keeping holiday. Drums beat, bands played, trumpets sounded, and mixed with the sounds of tipsy singing and laughter that continued till long past midnight; and just as things were growing quiet and we were getting drowsy, came a loud rat-tat-tat at our doors and the noise of Arab porters crying out, "La Diligence! La Diligence!"

CHAPTER XVII.

RAIN.—AN ENGLISH LADY'S OPINIONS ON THE ARABS.—WILD BIRDS.
—THE EARTHQUAKE.

AND the blessed rain came. We had heard it pattering and plashing between our dreams, and, when we came out into the open air, it was moist and sweet and cool. For the first time throughout our entire journey we were unable to procure the coupé to ourselves, for the assizes were to commence at Mostaganem, and, what with witnesses, lawyers, plaintiffs and defendants, the diligence was more than crowded.

We could not see our companion, but, from the large share of the coupé that he monopolized, we thought he must be a very stout person indeed; alas, how we had hoped and prayed that he might prove thin! But there was no help for it, and, by the time we began to be cramped in every limb, came the blessed, beautifying daylight and the ever-shifting African landscape, that made us forget everything else.

We forgave our fellow-traveller his burliness after a while, for he proved so full of information and pleasant. He was a barrister, and told us of all the most important cases coming off at Mostaganem, and a fearful list it was. By far the greater number of prisoners were Arabs charged with assassinations. We told this gentleman of what we had heard at Tclemcen.

"In one place," we said, "the Arabs are represented as harmless, improvable, mild: in another as the incarnation of villany. What *are* we to believe?"

"Well," he said, "the fact is this, the Arabs are *pauvres diables*, and they are poorer now than they were before we came—that is to say, the Bedouin, the shepherd and the cultivator of a little land is poorer—and the consequence is, they are led from theft to murder. When we stop to change horses every one will alight to take coffee, and you will see a couple of priests, one looking as

x

if he had just come out of a war-hospital. He was attacked near Tclemcen one evening, robbed, and left on the road for dead. That is one of the worst cases we have, though there are others of a piece with it. The priests ride on the box with the coachman, and in the rotunda are some Arabs who are going to witness on the side of the accused, one of them you must look at, too; he is dressed like a prince and has the face of *le diable*. He is the son of a Bach-Agha."

By-and-by, we came to a little roadside caravansary, and every one got out, the handsome, *nonchalant* Arabs and their "murdered man," among the rest. The poor curé looked very ill still, and had a gentlemanly, but shabby, appearance. The Bach-Agha's son was dressed in purple and fine raiment, and looked a king—till you saw his face closely—when he looked a very Mephistopheles. It was an indescribably cruel, clever, sensual face,—a face from which you turned with repugnance.

After passing through some very lovely tamarisk-groves, amid which wound a broad, bright river, a branch of the Chelif, we entered upon the vast monotonous plain of the Habra. These African plains are only varied here and there by shifting bands of road-makers, military posts, and by little French colonies or Arab douars; and when you commence your journey, you feel as if it would never end. You cross horizon after horizon. You see a white speck in the distance and say, "That must be our halting-place;" but, when you arrive, it is a military post and nothing more —the dogs rush out barking and yelling, French Zouaves, who stand basking in the sun, come up to ask for newspapers and letters; and the Spahis look at us whilst they smoke their paper cigarettes, and show their white teeth as they say "Bon jour." Then, after getting a glass of water or wine, the diligence moves slowly off, and we leave behind the glistening white post, the red-cloaked, brown-skinned Spahis, and the pack of dogs.

How hot it is! When we alight and walk a little way, ankle-deep in alpha grass and wild thyme, the leaves seem warm and dry as if the soil below were burning away with volcanic fire. We shall be sunburnt to the complexion of Moors before our journey is done, we say, and when inside the diligence, and pin up shawls and cloaks to keep out the wind that is as warm now as it was cold when we started. The plains have each a climate of their own, and travellers should always plan their journeys—as we did—to avoid crossing them at early morning or at night, when a terrible miasma arises from the soil and is never harmless, often as dangerous as poison.

Mostaganem is a lively little place, and on account of the assizes was full of strangers. Greatly to our amusement we encountered our stout *compagnon du voyage* on the evening of our arrival, as shrunk from his natural size as a rabbit after skinning. What strange metamorphose had changed him in so short a space from the size of a Falstaff to a lean and hungry-looking Cassius? It was very perplexing, but on a sudden it flashed on us like a revelation, that as all his luggage had consisted of a hat-box, and as he had doffed a thick grey travelling dress and donned a suit of shining black cloth, he must have carried his wardrobe on his back. It was very simple.

At Mostaganem I made the acquaintance of a countrywoman, the wife of a French gentleman holding a responsible official post there. Every one in Oran is sure to be an official if he is not in the army; and it is curious to see how the difference of calling modifies the political and social opinions. I never talked with a French officer who was not entirely opposed to the assimilation of races and incredulous of Arab civilization, nor with an official who was not equally enthusiastic about both. A *préfet*, a *sous-préfet*, a *maire*, or any other of the dozen gentlemen who administer justice and keep order in these French-African towns, is pretty sure to speak hopefully and humanely of the Arabs : a colonel or a commandant uses much the same tone about them as our officers up-country do regarding the Sepoys and Seedy-boys.

My countrywoman spoke of the Arabs with great sympathy.

" My heart bleeds for the poor people," she said : " think of what they have suffered during the past year ! They had planted their little bits of cornfields, and the corn was shooting up in abundance, when the locusts came in billions and trillions, and corn, potatoes, rye, everything was destroyed. They starve, or else they steal and fill our prisons and reformatories. People say, let them starve or work, but you cannot change the habits of a people in a day.

"Most of these poor things under trial now are Bedouins, as ignorant as savages from Timbuctoo. My husband told me yesterday of a poor little boy condemned to five years' imprisonment for having stolen a turkey! Do you suppose, Madame, that that boy will come out of his prison a better French subject than he went in? I have lived for years among the Arabs—in Constantine, in Algeria, in Oran—I have studied Arabic on purpose to hold intercourse with them and to be able to sympathize with and understand my husband's calling, and I have come to this conclusion—Madame, it is only by assimilation that the Arab is to be improved. There was a great outcry among the colonists after the Emperor had visited Africa in 1865, because he was said to show partiality to the Arab; but, good heavens, what a different position does the honest *colon* hold to the richest *indigène?* The *colon* is a Frenchman, and therefore a noble being; the *indigène* is an Arab, and what isn't good enough for an Arab? For my part, I think the Emperor was wise in taking that tone. I think the colonists have much to suffer, but the Arabs incontestably more, and if the Emperor did not take their part, who would ?"

We rested two nights at Mostaganem, and the blessed rain kept falling all the time, though no sooner were we on our way again, than the sun came out and all was bright and warm.

Our next halting place was Relizane. We reached Relizane in six hours' easy travelling through a monotonous country, part wild, part cultivated, with flocks of cranes feeding on the pastures, vultures and eagles flying overhead, coveys of partridges whirring from the brushwood, and hares scuttling across the road as we passed along. Whenever we passed an Arab village, a crowd of half, or wholly naked children ran down and followed us, calling out for coppers. They would run incredible distances thus, and when a coin was thrown out, there would be a diving of little black polls in the grass, a momentary scramble, then all was ready to start afresh. Those who are fortunate enough to get the money, put it in their mouths—having no clothes they could clearly have no pockets—and, if not as comfortable, it was certainly a safe and convenient mode of carrying their spoils.

My journey properly ends at Relizane, since this is the last halting-place in Oran, the last Spanish province of Algeria. But we set foot on Algerian soil just as the first shock of earthquake had spread a panic throughout the length and breadth of the country, and I will give a page or two to that most terrible time.

Never shall I forgot our journey from Relizane to Algiers. We were happily under no apprehension about those dear to us at Algiers, as we had received telegrams from them assuring us of their safety, but every one we met had some fearful story to tell of the loss of life and property in the villages of the Metidja. We knew these villages well, having spent many days there not twelve months back; and our hearts failed us at the thought of what we were now to see in place of the peace and plenty we had seen then.

The first town within the devastated circle, Milianah, stood intact, though the prevailing panic was something indescribable. All the women were looking white and wan, some had lost friends and relatives in the Metidja, others had taken to their beds from sheer fright, a few awaited a final shock which was to be the 'crack of doom.' Wherever we went we heard descriptions of the terrible event, all more or less exaggerated. According to one, the Zakkar, a mountain as high as Snowdon rising to the north of Milianah, had rocked to and fro, emitting flames of fire; according to another, many houses had been split and shaken by the shock.

If the former account were true, we found the mouth of the Zakkar shut close enough, and its sides had grown marvellously green again since the catastrophe, though happening only a few days back. We walked round and round the town and saw no houses that had taken any harm. The shock was, nevertheless, awful, as we gathered from the plain, unvarnished account given us by the prefêt. He had expected at the time nothing more nor less than the entire destruction of Milianah.

The shock had been severely felt at Algiers and Blidah, but it was a little cluster of villages in the Metidja, by name, Bou-kika, Mouzaiaville,

El-Affrom, and La Chiffa, that had suffered most. Our way lay straight through that village; and so recent was the calamity, and so inaccurate the accounts of it, that we set off to Algiers without in the least knowing where we could break the journey. Some people said, "Bou-kika is unharmed; you will find every accommodation at Bou-kika;" others said, "You will have to go right to Blidah, and break your journey there. Blidah is recovering itself, and you will find the hotels much the same as if nothing had happened." A third said, "Blidah is as empty as a plundered place. There isn't a crust of bread to be had there."

In this uncertainty we set off. It was a superb moonlight night, and as we passed along, we saw woeful things.

We had talked of sleeping at Bou-kika, but Bou-kika was as dead and silent as if death were in every dwelling. Every one, in fact, was encamped outside the village, and a knot of soldiers, gathered round a watch-fire, guarded the deserted houses. Here the ruin had been partial; but soon we came to great, ghastly spectres of what, a week ago, had been thriving little towns—each with its church, its hotel, its shops and cafés. Here and there, above great heaps of brick and mortar, stood out a chimney, a wall, or a doorway, or, indeed, a whole house, split like a pomegranate; but the place had collapsed like a child's card-house. One must tread upon the heels of an earthquake to understand what it is—the suddenness of it—the despair of it—the desolation of it.*

More than a hundred souls had been buried alive here; and what testifies to the paralysing nature of the shock is the great proportion of young children. Mothers were so horrified that they rushed out of doors, leaving their sleeping babies behind!

We reached Blidah early in the morning, and found the town as deserted as if stricken by a plague. The large, prosperous hotel where we had often stayed before, was shut up. The streets were

---

* It is hardly necessary to say that everything that liberality, active and passive, could do, was done, and done at once, for the sufferers by the earthquake. Nothing was spared, money, counsel, sympathy, and, I have no doubt that by this time, the villages mentioned are rebuilt and re-inhabited.

silent, the shops were all closed; thankful enough were we to get a little coffee and a morsel of bread at a little cabaret before taking the early train to Algiers. All Blidah was encamped outside the town, and the long lines of tents, and the unwonted aspect of hundreds of wealthy families turned out of house and home, and shifting for themselves in the best way they could, was sad and strange. It was breakfast-time. Coffee was boiling on every little camp-fire, children were running about borrowing a neighbour's cup or pitcher; ladies were making their toilettes as best they could; men were wandering hither and thither, smoking away their disturbed thoughts.

The Arabs alone looked unmoved. "It is the will of God," they say when any evil happens, and they resign themselves to it, outwardly calm as statues.

In about an hour and a half we reached Algiers. The weather was glorious; and as we drove up to the well-known villa on the green height of Mustapha Supérieure, and looked down upon the bright, blue sea, and the glistening shore, and the white Moorish city crowning the sunny Sahel, we said that Spain had showed us no fairer prospect.

And yet we were sorry—who would not be?—that our journey had come to an end. May all those who follow in our track find the same bright skies and pleasant faces, and bring home from Spain and Oran as many happy memories as we did.

www.ingramcontent.com/pod-product-compliance
Lightning Source LLC
Chambersburg PA
CBHW030751230426
43667CB00007B/922